LIFE WITHOUT ELGAR

This is a study of what for Edward Elgar may have been a lifelong obsession with a youthful passion; Variation 13 of the Enigma Variations, composed nearly two decades after the affair, may have been inspired by the object of that love, who after the engagement was broken off emigrated to New Zealand.

The book is based on the device of imagining that throughout their lives Edward Elgar and the girl with whom he fell in love, Helen Weaver, exchanged letters from across the globe. The author Ann Merivale believes in reincarnation and feels that in a previous life she was Helen Weaver.

Readers must judge for themselves whether Ms Merivale has caught the spirit of Elgar's thought processes and epistolatory style. This is a novel approach to biography and a daring one.
Humphrey Burton, Writer and Broadcaster

Dr Roger Woolger, to whose ground-breaking work in past-life therapy this book refers, and for whom music played a vital part in the nourishment of the soul, would have very much relished the insights, not only into the life of Elgar and his relationships, but also the connections between different lives and eras which this interesting and unusual book provides.
Jane May, Programme Director, Woolger Institute

One of the aspects of past life theory, for which there is much supportive evidence, is that time as we know it does not exist, and it is possible to remember and relive the past as if were happening now through the medium of Deep Memory Process, as Dr Woolger called it.

In writing the many letters contained in the book the author appears to have used psychic powers combined with past life technique to connect with, and actually become, the writers of the letters, as if their hands wielded the pen.

The letters make wonderful sense if one knows about Sir Edward William

Elgar's life and become truly astounding if one remembers the process by which the letters may have been written. It is as though the original people can now say what they perhaps were unable to say at the time, and to rewrite that which has been lost in order that we might have a better understanding of the past which surrounded Elgar's life.

Having known the author since we trained together with Dr Roger Woolger nearly twenty years ago I can vouch for her absolute honesty, integrity, and sincerity, and her extensive personal knowledge of past life experiences both her own and those of her many colleagues and clients.

A fascinating and enlightening easy read.

Brian Weld, Woolger training

Ann Merivale's intimate account of her love for Edward Elgar's work in her current life, and the passionate involvement with both man and music in a previous life, is deeply personal, insightful and touching. In spite of the factual research contained in this book and a few academic musings, Ann's journey of musical self-discovery is clearly guided by the heart. She trusts and follows her feelings, which is the only way to access what is usually hidden from the conscious mind: true self-knowledge, wisdom and healing. Ann's book elucidates what holistic therapists encounter with clients every day: healing is a process inseparable from the soul's journey through various embodiments. Rather than being an outlandish theory, reincarnation actually constitutes the practical framework of healing. It lends universal meaning, purpose and value to human life as we know it while in a body.

Sascha Kriese, M.A.Litt, Ayurvedic health-care practitioner, pulse reader, Shadow Work® coach, and formerly theatre director.

I have been incredibly moved by this beautiful book and only stopped reading to make a cup of tea before rushing back to it. Having attended many courses given by Roger Woolger, the famed Jungian psychotherapist who was also the author's teacher, I fully appreciate the healing gained from his work, which she expounds so well. When it came to the letters in Part II, it really didn't seem to me like Ann Merivale writing, but all the time like Helen and Edward. The book all rings so true, and several times I was moved to tears, particularly over references to the violin concerto, which I love even more than the cello concerto.

Audrey Williams, is currently Director of Music at a church in Exmouth. A lifelong musician, and being an organist as well a retired teacher of piano and violin, she has a profound knowledge of the music of J.S. Bach and also that of Elgar.

I have no expertise in the field of regression and am personally open minded on the subject of reincarnation, but the author of this book appears undoubtedly to bear witness to the efficacy of Deep Memory Process therapy. Elgar was a fascinating man, both musically and psychologically, and the many hints he dropped about hidden messages in, for instance, the Enigma Variations do make it possible to believe that memories of his first love continued re-surfacing in both his thoughts and his music. The notion that Elgar and Helen Weaver continued their 'relationship' after her departure from England – indeed after both their deaths – is appealing, and would doubtless prove intriguing to sceptics as well as to believers. Ann Merivale is also at pains to stress that her book is chiefly about healing, and that the reader is free to question her belief in her previous incarnation as Helen. What does emerge loud and clear from the book is her own deep love of the music and, with that as a starting point, she has written a useful intro-duction to Elgar for beginners at the same as constructing a fascinating, speculative, 'alternative' view of the life of one of England's finest composers.

Dr. Richard Kershaw, taught Music at Sherborne School in Dorset for many years, having previously held a lecturing post in the Music Department of Aberdeen University. Himself a cellist, he has a profound knowledge of the life and works of Sir Edward Elgar. Now in semi-retirement, he has published numerous compositions, mainly for the enjoyment of young instrumental students, and many of these feature on examination board syllabuses all over the world.

Although the field of Deep Memory Regression is something about which I remain sceptical, I accept the author's sincere desire to heal people through its application, and I empathise very much with her desire to support the Elgar Birthplace Museum. Her early life is very interesting and fluently expressed, and her affinity with the person and music of Elgar is undeniable. The photographs of some of Elgar and Helen's supposed favourite haunts are an added attraction.

Lucy Bowen, Soprano and Head of Vocal Studies at Hereford Sixth Form College

As an imaginative reconstruction, the letters between Edward Elgar and Helen Weaver which form part of this book are an admirable achievement, managing to give an impression of a relationship much in the manner of the epistolary novel – a form I believe is still as valid as ever.

The author's love for Elgar – the man and his music – comes through movingly, and the way she splices details of her own life and her exploration of Elgar together makes this into an interesting narrative.

Simon Rees, writer and lecturer who spent 23 years as Welsh National Opera's dramaturg.

For Elgarians of a romantic nature this book is full of "food for thought", with many lovely set pieces to feed the reader's imagination.

Wendy Hill, Volunteer worker at the Elgar Birthplace Museum and speaker on Elgar.

The subject of the Thirteenth Enigma Variation has for long been a matter of debate. Whether or not this book gives us the answer can also be debated, but it is at least an interesting and enjoyable read.

Chris Bennett, Supervisor, Elgar Birthplace Museum

I found this book most stimulating and interesting. Whilst some of the areas covered in the book may make difficult – even uncomfortable – reading for many, Ann has not been afraid to delve deeply into the spiritual side of art and life. I'm sure that putting her thoughts into words was a huge challenge and she has succeeded in writing a book never less than thought provoking.

Simon Watterton, concert pianist, teacher and chamber music coach.

For Linda & Fernandez -
with happy memories of the 2016 Leipzig
Bach Festival, and greatly hoping that you find

Life
Without
Elgar

A Tale of a Journeying Soul

this interesting & enjoyable.

Blessings,

cunmerivale@ bt. internet. com

Life
Without
Elgar

A Tale of a Journeying Soul

Ann Merivale

Winchester, UK
Washington, USA

First published by Sixth Books, 2014

Sixth Books is an imprint of John Hunt Publishing Ltd., Laurel House, Station Approach, Alresford, Hants, SO24 9JH, UK

office1@jhpbooks.net

www.johnhuntpublishing.com

www.6th-books.com

For distributor details and how to order please visit the 'Ordering' section on our website.

Text copyright: Ann Merivale 2013

ISBN: 978 1 78279 526 1

A CIP catalogue record for this book is available from the British Library.

Design: Stuart Davies
Cover image: Rowan Taliesin, www.rowantaliesin.co.uk

Printed and bound by CPI Group (UK) Ltd, Croydon, CR0 4YY

We operate a distinctive and ethical publishing philosophy in all areas of our business, from our global network of authors to production and worldwide distribution.

CONTENTS

For David, my constant critic, support, companion in music appreciation and the father of my three wonderful children.

Acknowledgements

I am as always grateful to so many people for helping me to birth this book. Trusting that I do not make too many serious omissions, here are those who come to my mind most strongly:

Dr John Harcup, Chairman of the West Midlands Branch of the Elgar Society, for his wonderful talks on EE.

Ernie Kay, for his general support of all things musical in the Malvern area and without whom none of these West Midlands events would occur.

Chris Bennett, and all the volunteers at the Elgar Birthplace Museum for all their hard work and for providing such a congenial venue for the above-mentioned talks. I am also grateful to Chris, the Supervisor of the Birthplace Museum, for answering many of my questions and for the suggestion made in EE's letter of 4 July 1904 re Alice's reasons for their frequent house moves. It was Carice, Elgar and Alice's daughter, who succeeded in procuring the birthplace cottage for the nation, and the Museum was opened in 2000.

Dr Donald Hunt, for his numerous excellent talks on various fascinating musical topics, given in aid of the Elgar Birthplace Musuem.

Timothy Day, the present owner of the ground floor of Plas Gwyn, Hereford, for his occasional invitations to his abode for fascinating talks and discussions in what was Elgar's study, followed by delicious teas. Elgar's First Symphony, The Kingdom, the Violin Concerto and the Introduction and Allegro for Strings were all written at Plas Gwyn. Timothy also, since they were considerably better than mine, kindly provided some of his own photos of Plas Gwyn.

Stephen Johnson for his wonderful insights into Elgar's music. I am indebted to him for the comment about "walking music" in

EE's letter of 12 March 1906, made in an excellent talk that he gave at the 2012 Three Choirs Festival in Hereford.

Simon Rees also has great insight into Elgar's music, and he talked about his soft spot for the military (mentioned in EE's Letter of 4 August 1916) in a fascinating talk on *Falstaff* given at the 2013 Three Choirs Festival.

Andrew Neil, a former Chairman of the Elgar Society, for his interesting talk on 'Elgar, India and Empire', upon which I also drew.

For the information on 'Rodey' in one of EE's letters, I strongly recommend a newly published book by John E. Kelly, entitled *ELGAR'S BEST FRIEND – Alfred Rodewald of Liverpool*, Carnegie Publishing Ltd., 2013.

It was the composer Anthony Powers who pointed out, in a talk given at Plas Gwyn on 18 May 2013, the apparent seamless quality of EE's music, mentioned in EE's letter of 12 March 1906. He compared it to that of Stravinsky, which he said was "so much more obviously a mosaic." This rang a big chord with me, as I feel that my own writing process is often similar to Elgar's composing – particularly when I am writing up a person's story by patching together notes that I have taken from therapy sessions or interviews.

For the information about Vera Hockman, Elgar's last love, I am indebted both to John Bridcut's marvellous film, *Elgar – the Man Behind the Mask*, and Kevin Allen for his book *Elgar in Love and the Third Symphony*, 2000 (on sale at the Elgar Birthplace Museum). In Helen's letter of 2 June 1930, I have re-quoted his quote from Vera Hockman's diaries. However, the conclusion that the two of them are twin souls is entirely my own. Had I known about Vera earlier, I would have discussed the point in my book *SOULS UNITED – The Power of Divine Connection* (published by Llewellyn Worldwide, USA, in 2009).

In Helen's same letter of 2 June 1930, she also talks about 'soul groups'. For more on this subject I strongly recommend the books of Dr Michael Newton, published by Llewellyn Worldwide, USA. Newton is a distinguished past life regression therapist who specialised in exploring the 'in-between life' state in great detail.

Lawrence, for always keeping me at it, for constantly challenging me, and for first suggesting that my Elgar theme merited a book all on its own.

My fellow 'Mouliners' for helping me to make the discovery about my previous life as Helen Weaver, and for, quite independently, endorsing that suggestion.

Wendy and Bernard Hill for organising the 'Elgar Jaunts' and other social events so competently.

Mr and Mrs M. Smalley for generously opening their home, Minafon, to the West Midlands Branch of the Elgar Society, and organising a lovely concert for us in their sitting room. This jaunt in June 2013 gave us the opportunity to appreciate the spot in Wales where Elgar enjoyed holidays with his close friend Alfred Rodewald.

My brother John, David, Lawrence, Sascha, Lucy, Richard, Wendy and Peter all made invaluable editorial comments and/or corrections.

And last but my no means least, Rowan Taliesin for her meticulous adherence to my instructions for the cover painting, combined of course with her own flashes of inspiration.

Introduction

On ne voit bien qu'avec le coeur; l'essentiel est invisible pour les yeux.
Antoine de St. Exupéry, Le Petit Prince

When Kevin Coates, the distinguished British artist, goldsmith and musician, commented to Rob Cowan on Radio Three's *Essential Classics* in March 2013 that "Mozart seemed to be ready formed when he was born", I don't know to what extent he was aware of the truth of his statement. I have been a practitioner of Deep Memory Process (or past life regression) therapy since 1998, as well as writing on related spiritual subjects since 1993, and people in my field take it completely for granted that a genius such as Mozart – or indeed the renowned English composer Sir Edward Elgar (1857–1934) – were only able to achieve what they did because of having been musicians many times before. Sathya Sai Baba, the great Indian *avatar*[1] and my own *guru*[2] in my present lifetime, took this still further. In a conversation with some of his devotees, he once said that there was no such thing as genius – that what others see as someone's 'genius' was actually no more than the result of their having had a great deal of practice at the métier concerned in previous lives. When someone then asked him about Mozart, his reply was that, in all the incarnations he had ever had, Mozart had never chosen to do anything but music. (Sai Baba had extraordinary powers of clairvoyance and could read everybody's past, present and future.)

To many Westerners this may well seem strange, or even absurd, but we should note that well over half of the world's population believes in reincarnation. Furthermore, Dr Ian Stevenson (1918–2007), of the University of Virginia School of Medicine, travelled extensively for forty years investigating

3,000 cases of children who claimed to remember past lives. His 300 papers and fourteen books give very convincing evidence of reincarnation for, when the children involved located their previous abode, their story would be confirmed by people they identified as former relatives. Also, Stevenson's major, two-volume, work[3] documents 200 cases of birthmarks that correspond with a wound inflicted on the deceased person whose life the child recalled.

To Christians I can point out that belief in multiple lives was widespread in the early Church, until its suppression at the Council of Constantinople in AD 553. The instigator of the suppression was the powerful Empress Theodora, wife of Justinian, who disliked the idea of returning to Earth as anything other than an Empress. The Pope at the time of this Council was in prison, and the motion was passed by only three votes. The Bible was then expurgated of most of its references to reincarnation.

I myself, having been brought up strongly Catholic, took a very long time to come round to my present beliefs, but, having done so, it occurred to me that the notion of reincarnation and karma (the law of cause and effect) was the only way of explaining how God could be totally just. For otherwise how can it be fair that some people are born with a silver spoon in their mouth while others have to endure great hardship or poverty? Or that some have very short lives and others long ones? And how could we possibly learn all that we need to learn in a single lifetime? Experiencing every aspect of life in this world enables us to become fully rounded personalities.

The first trigger was a lecture I heard in 1991 about the American *Christian* clairvoyant, Edgar Cayce.[4] I then embarked upon many years of extensive research into the subject and found the evidence to be incontrovertible. Cayce, who died in 1945, had prophesied both the world wars as well as numerous other things such as the date of the first moon landing, and he cured hundreds of people all over the world through his 'medical readings' given in trance. The remedies that he prescribed are still widely used today and, once he had worked out a philosophy of reincarnation that was completely in accord with his Christianity, he also gave numerous 'past life readings', which again helped large numbers of people.

To believe or not to believe: that is the question. Or need it be? How much does it really matter? We all have different paths, just as we have different talents and interests; were this not so, society could not function. I recently read Janice Galloway's novel about Clara Schumann,[5] which enthralled me. So vivid did I find her account that I felt sure that the author must herself be a reincarnation of Clara. On the other hand, others reading that book, who did not share my beliefs, would doubtless class it as 'fiction', 'fantasy', 'vivid imagination' or a mixture of all three. Yet these differing viewpoints need not prevent us from all enjoying Galloway's novel equally.

This little book of mine has been prompted by a past life regression that I did in 2012, in which – to my intense surprise – I found myself as Helen Weaver, Edward Elgar's first love and fiancée. I am not setting out to prove this particular 'discovery' (which it would be impossible for me to do anyway), but simply to explain how Deep Memory Process therapy (DMP) has helped me in my personal journey. I put the word 'discovery' in quotes partly to reflect the scepticism with which I anticipate it being greeted by some, if not many, readers; partly because, a full twelve months on I am myself still reeling from it. I can perhaps expect other Elgar lovers to accuse me of wishful thinking, but I assure anyone who might want to do this that being the person to have caused EE's first heartbreak by leaving him for a new life in New Zealand is the very *last* thing that I would have wished for! Yet, I have found on reflection that this therapy session explains so much about my present life that it is difficult for me to disbelieve what I experienced in that regression.

To those who find this philosophy difficult or impossible to accept I feel it important to stress that as therapists in this field we have no interest in proving reincarnation, but simply in resolving issues that are troubling people in their present lives. These can be physical, mental or emotional, and my own main teacher, the distinguished Jungian psychotherapist, Dr Roger Woolger (d. November 2011) ably expounded the healing methods that he developed in his major book.[6] My own first book,[7] which, like this one, is largely autobiographical, also aimed to demonstrate how DMP works in practice, but I will nevertheless now briefly give some illustrative examples of the very satisfactory results that I have so frequently experienced through this, often extremely challenging, work.

A woman whom I will call Carol came to me some years ago with a list of physical symptoms that had been troubling her for a long time. The worst of these was chronic headaches, but she also had a great deal of discomfort in her left upper arm. In the first regression that we did she found herself as a soldier on a battlefield, who was killed by a bullet going through his neck. After the death I took her, as is the common practice in DMP, into what is known as the *Bardo* (a Tibetan word that literally means 'between islands'). There, besides helping her to find out what had been the lessons she had learnt from that lifetime, I got her to visualise angels (her own choice) removing the bullet physically and then filling the hole with a beautiful colour. The headaches then ceased and never, so far as I know, returned. At the next session Carol saw that the same bullet had entered her left upper arm before penetrating her neck. So we repeated the process in the *Bardo*, this time focusing on the arm, which then also healed.

Lynn, a client whose problems were more emotional than physical, wanted to know why she was unable to maintain relationships with men for very long, however much she loved the partner concerned. Gradually we found this to have been a repeated pattern over a number of lifetimes, and it also became clear that she had never been able to love herself and consequently felt unworthy of the man of her choice. Her partners had obviously been picking up her expectations of rejection, subconsciously at least, and this had caused them all in due course to leave. In her present life Lynn's father had never shown her any love and she helped herself to break the pattern by doing some 'inner child' work (championed particularly well by the American therapist John Bradshaw[8]) and in due course learning to see herself as the attractive, desirable woman that she was. She is now happily married and expecting her second child.

Sceptics who know only a little about this form of therapy sometimes comment that people who go in for it are hoping to discover themselves as having been, for instance, Cleopatra or Napoleon in a previous life. Well, firstly going in for it out of pure curiosity is always to be discouraged, and secondly, in all my years of practice, I have only ever found one former Roman Emperor (name not revealed). In his case that particular life made perfect sense, and revisiting it with my assistance enabled the client concerned to resolve an issue of power with which he had been struggling for some time.

Many of the past lives that are revealed through DMP are distinctly drab and boring, many are traumatic, many are what Woolger often described as "lives of quiet desperation". An excellent example of this last can be seen in François Mauriac's novel *Thérèse Desqueyroux*, recently made into a very well-acted film starring Audrey Tautou. Thérèse, who was brought up in a family in which it was not permissible to feel feelings, still less to show them, and who married into another family where this was equally the case, didn't understand what had led her into the crime that she committed. Nowadays, a century later, such attitudes towards showing feelings are fortunately less prevalent, but it is still a fact that most people who survive severe mental pain do so by cutting off from their feelings. This may not often lead one into crime, but feelings have to go somewhere and suppressing them may be a factor contributing to disease or serious illness.

Although I say that we don't look for proof of past lives, that doesn't mean that confirmation never happens. When I hadn't been living in Shropshire for very long, I regressed Sarah to a life as a maid in a castle. At one point I happened to ask her if she could tell me the name of the castle (a thing we don't normally bother with), and she replied "Hopton". Neither of us had heard of it, but a couple of weeks later I was on a coach tour as part of Ludlow Festival and the guide pointed out the ruins of Hopton Castle. So I phoned Sarah the next day to tell her and she was absolutely thrilled. I, however, was even more delighted that the regression had enabled her to release her feelings of "always working terribly hard without being appreciated".

Many past life regression therapists induce a state of trance in their clients by the use of hypnotherapy, but Woolger preferred not to use hypnosis because he believed it to cause dissociation from what was being seen; he found results to be better when his clients were fully "in the life" rather than simply observing it like a film. He taught his students that reliving trauma was the best way of clearing it permanently and consequently being able to move forward in ways that were previously unprecedented for them. Working "from the body" was his particular, though not exclusive, speciality, and a couple of his oft-repeated phrases were, "The *body* remembers", "The body can't lie". I shall be saying a bit more about this later, because it was my body that took me into Helen Weaver's life.

Most people who come for a DMP session have a particular issue (or often several) that they want to deal with; many come as a last resort after conventional and/or other therapies have failed to resolve their problem(s). We always of course set out to look for the root of people's most burning issue, but getting there straight away can never be guaranteed. The reason for this is that the subconscious always knows what is best for our healing and what we most need to let go of. Sometimes what comes up is a big surprise (as in my own case with Helen Weaver), but the reason for it is invariably made apparent to the client, even if not instantly. Sometimes there are other things that need to be cleared before they are ready to tackle the burning issue that has brought them for the therapy; these can sometimes date from childhood in a person's present life. A further point worth noting is that belief in reincarnation is by no means essential for the therapy to be successful.

In my third book,[9] I wrote in some detail about the process of reincarnating, explaining the various steps, the choices that are made in advance and so on. So here I will just mention briefly that it is not the *whole being* that descends each time into a new body. People use different terminology, but I like to follow the tradition of calling the journeying part the 'soul', while the 'spirit' (often referred to as the Higher Self) as the part of you that remains on the other side, giving guidance when necessary. At the end of each new lifetime the soul returns to its Higher Self, and the new learning that has been gained on Earth is absorbed by the spirit and retained for future use.

A strong feature of present-day Western society is that people are taught to put things into clearly labelled boxes: true or false, scientifically proven or 'hypothesis or fantasy', black or white, profit or loss-making... I could go on indefinitely. It was not always so. The medicine men (and women!) of yore were the shamans/priests/healers who communed with the world of spirit. Modern medicine does of course work wonders (I could myself be right now 'on the way out' if my breast cancer had not been nipped in the bud last year, and I have a close friend whose daughter has just had a heart transplant), yet at the same time more and more people are now turning to holistic medicine, which treats the whole person and looks *for* causes rather than *at* symptoms. While being grateful for the GPs and surgeons who sorted out my broken hip in 1997 as well as my breast lump in

2012, I personally prefer my general health to be cared for by a homoeopath/osteopath and an Ayurvedic practitioner. The former has known my husband and me for many years and, if we both have, for instance, a bad cold or 'flu, he is likely to prescribe us each a different remedy. This is because, though we have a lot in common, we are very different both physically and mentally. Shamanism is also at present very much on the up in Europe and America.

The great Elizabethan, Dr John Dee, was renowned as an astronomer and a mathematician, but he was also expert in astrology, and he communicated with angels through a medium named Edward Kelley. In fact he studied and wrote in his journals about the 'Enochian language' (the language of angels. The name comes from Dee's assertion that the prophet Enoch had been the last human being before Kelley and himself to know the angelic language). For Dee none of these disciplines was any less 'scientific' than the others. Much more recently, C. G. Jung, who surely had one of the greatest minds of the twentieth century, was expert in astrology besides being the father of much of modern psychoanalysis and psychiatry. However, while having been regarded by his contemporaries as a 'mystic', he himself always wanted to be seen as a scientist.

When I mentioned Jung just now, I had to check myself because I was on the point of describing him as "one of the greatest minds..." James Cochrane (whose book[10] came as a godsend to me, a Romance linguist with also a great love of my mother tongue) strongly advocates precision as well as grammatical correctness in the English language. Had I written what first came into my head, Cochrane would no doubt have pointed out that Carl Gustav Jung was much more than a mind. The same applies to you and me. A very popular phrase these days is "thinking outside the box", but my question is – why do we have to put everything into boxes in the first place? Going back to you, since you no doubt know more about yourself than about Jung: what do you consist of? Flesh, blood, bones, a heart and a brain, which would cause your body to die if they ceased working... Yes, but is that all? Aren't your mind, your thoughts, your hopes and aspirations, your dreams, your moods ... all equally important aspects of *you*? Does each of these have to be put into a separate box from each of the others?

The first part of this book, which consists of three fairly brief chapters, is autobiographical. I make no apology for this because I see an explanation of how I came to my present beliefs as important for understanding my story. The middle section, which of the three is likely to be the most interesting for music lovers, consists of imagined correspondence between Sir Edward Elgar and Helen Weaver. The final section, which includes my purely personal thoughts about some of my favourite music, is focused mainly on the healing that DMP therapy has given me.

Returning to boxes and individual beliefs, let me say something about Helen's first 'imagined' letter to her beloved. As I was writing it, I felt myself to actually *be* Helen (apologies for the split infinitive!); I was putting into words the feelings that I had experienced a year earlier when I did the regression with my Woolger colleagues. (N.B. In DMP therapy we always pay more attention to feelings and emotions than to facts because it is there that healing is needed.) People reading this letter who find the idea of my having previously been Helen Weaver either hard or impossible to swallow can interpret it as pure – or perhaps even wild – imagination. But there is also a third way in which it could be seen: Helen's dilemma – to follow her heart or her reason – is a common one, and the steps taken are likely to have long-term consequences. If you have never been faced with having to make a comparably difficult decision, you are either unusual, lucky or (probably) both. So this letter could be taken purely symbolically, as representing one of the many aspects of the human condition.

As well as my colleagues who guided me into and through

the regression, I need to thank Cora Weaver for her research in New Zealand, from which I gained factual additions to what I saw in my regression in May 2012. I discovered her book[11] only some months later, found in it nothing that contradicted my experience, but owe Cora a huge debt in some of the little details of what I have recounted. She has, however, told me in an email that she is now working on an amplified, corrected, version of this now out of print book; her original research, carried out in the 1980s, has been superseded by certain more precise facts. But, since her research has necessarily been into facts rather than feelings, I am not concerned as to how it might affect my own account. (Her new book will certainly be worth looking out for!)

As for EE's letters, I stress that I have made no attempt at all to mimic his style. Unlike Anthony Payne,[12] I am not even remotely qualified to do this. EE was a born writer, while I only started writing when I felt that I had things I needed to say, and furthermore I couldn't possibly emulate EE's wonderful humour. Still less could I even attempt to add sketches to the letters. (My mother's artistic gift skipped a generation and was passed on to my daughter, Alice. In childhood she lived very much in her own little wonderland, but now in adulthood she exhibits just the same strength of character and level-headedness as her other namesake, EE's wife!) Even the most serious of writers and therapists are permitted – nay, even *need* for their health – to enjoy themselves from time to time. So I trust that Elgarians and musicologists will take 'EE's letters', with my occasional bits of fun, in that spirit rather than dwelling on any possible inaccuracies or saying that I have put some unlikely words into Edward Elgar's mouth. I am neither an academic nor a musicologist, but a linguist turned writer and therapist.

So too, ye music historians, however much delight it would give you to prove me wrong, please don't bother to go rushing off to check the records of, for instance, concerts in Auckland at the end of 1905. I have allowed myself some artist's licence and trust that you will too. Although I saw a clear picture of myself as Helen attending a concert at which the *Enigma Variations* were performed and felt it to be in Auckland, I recognise that, while I have been trained to trust feelings, others are trained to do precisely the opposite. And, were I to think for a moment outside my own particular box, it is even possible (though it didn't *feel* like it to me) that I as Ann was remembering a performance of this wonderful work that I very likely heard as a teenager at the Colston Hall in Bristol.

This brings me to another question that is sometimes asked about the therapy: how can one tell when something is real or when it is false memory or purely imagined? The simplest answer is, I think, that the experienced therapist can easily tell the difference between 'real' and 'unreal' simply because they *feel* different when the regression is taking place. Also, the client's healing will be more profound and more lasting when something completely genuine has been shed. Here is an example from my personal experience on one of my Woolger training workshops. I was taken into a slave life in America, where I had a particularly cruel master who beat me repeatedly. At a point when I was in pain from a beating and had been just about left for dead, Roger happened to come round to see how my fellow student, who was acting as the therapist, was faring. He asked me what happened next: whether I died or whether I recovered and carried on working on the plantation. I was then much less practised at getting into past lives than I am now, and I had not so long beforehand paid a visit to the Liverpool Slavery Museum, where I had been very taken by the stories of former slaves who did so much to put an end to the Slave Trade. Being unable to see exactly what happened after my master had left me in that dreadful state, I visualised an escape and making a new, better life for myself in Europe. Roger, however, felt sure that this was 'fabrication' (or wishful thinking!) on my part and so, once he had made me face up to the reality of having died as a result of all the beatings, I was able to let go permanently of my long-held 'slave mentality'. But as a general rule, since one is normally guided by one's Higher Self, subconscious or intuition (whichever one prefers to call it), one can learn to trust one's feelings, appreciating that they are the best guide as to what one needs to look at.

In contrast to my own little slave story, another workshop participant had throughout his life had a terrible fear of heights. When Roger was using him to demonstrate on, we all joined in at the point when he was surrounded by a mocking crowd. This crowd ended up pushing him into a well (which can be made to feel *very* realistic when there are a number of people partici-pating!), and after his death Roger did some powerful therapy with him. The very next day, during a break, a group of us went for a walk together near a cliff edge, and the man who had "drowned in the well" went right up to the edge of the cliff and looked over it completely fearlessly – a thing he had never previ-ously been able to do.

I hope now to have made clear that the idea behind this little book is NOT to convince anybody that I was Helen Weaver in one of my previous lives. Whether I was or was not is of secondary concern. This book is concerned primarily with healing, for which the therapist can never be more than a catalyst. For, just so long as we don't destroy it completely in the very near future, our precious world will be healed once everyone in it has healed themselves. And my aim here, which I also hope to have already made clear, is twofold. I want to cross boundaries between two disciplines that (to my mind sadly) tend normally to be separate: the therapeutic/healing/spiritual world and that of music. After all, does not music itself cross boundaries? And is it not well known for its therapeutic and healing properties? At the same time I am hoping to offer to Elgarians and other music lovers some information on spiritual subjects that may be new to them, and to tell people who already share my spiritual interests, but know little or nothing about Elgar, something – hopefully in a readable and enjoyable way – about his life and music.

So, with the Little Prince, I urge readers to consider my tale not with your eyes and intellects, but with your *hearts*. At the start of the Kyrie, which opens his *Missa Solemnis*, Beethoven wrote, "Vom Herzen, möge es wieder, zu Herzen gehen!", which can be translated as "From the heart, may it go to the heart", and EE's close friend Alfred Rodewald used to say to him, "You compose from the heart, not only from the brain". Music lovers, like poets, are probably better able than many people to understand the Little Prince's assertion that the essential things in life are to be seen not with the eyes, but with the heart. The rest is all explained in my text and my only desires are that you will firstly enjoy it and secondly remain open to the possibility of at least some of it being true.

Notes

1. The word avatar means 'divine descent'. While Christians believe that Jesus is the world's only ever divine incarnation, India has had many such: for instance Rama, Krishna, and more recently the triple incarnation of Sai Baba of Shirdi (who, when he died in 1918, said that he would return eight years later), Sathya Sai Baba (1926–2011), and his predicted successor, Prema Sai. As well as performing countless healings and other astounding miracles, Sathya Sai Baba founded numerous educational institutions, hospitals, welfare and clean water projects, and an 'Education in Human Values' system, which has spread through numerous schools throughout the world.
2. The word *guru* literally means 'remover of darkness'.
3. The shorter version of this massive work, written in 1997 for the general reader, is entitled *Where Reincarnation and Biology Intersect*.

4. See, for instance, *The Story of Edgar Cayce – There is a River,* Thomas Sugrue, ARE Press, USA, *A Seer Out of Season,* Harmon Hartzell Bro, Ph.D., Signet, USA and *EDGAR CAYCE: The Sleeping Prophet,* Jess Stearn, Bantam, 1997.

5. *CLARA,* Janice Galloway, Vintage, 2003.

6. *OTHER LIVES, OTHER SELVES – A Jungian Psychotherapist discovers Past Lives,* Roger Woolger, Ph.D., Doubleday, USA, 1987.

7. *KARMIC RELEASE – Journeying Back to the Self,* Ann Merivale, Sai Towers Publications, India, 2006.

8. *HOMECOMING – Reclaiming and Championing Your Inner Child,* John Bradshaw, Piatkus, 1999.

9. *DISCOVERING THE LIFE PLAN – Eleven Steps to Your Destiny,* Ann Merivale, O-Books, 2012.

10. *BETWEEN YOU AND I – A Little Book of **Bad** English,* James Cochrane, with an Introduction by John Humphrys, Icon Books Ltd., 2004.

11. *THE THIRTEENTH ENIGMA? – The Story of Edward Elgar's Early Love,* Cora Weaver, Thames Publishing, London, 1988.

12. The composer Anthony Payne completed Elgar's third symphony from the sketches that he had made before he died.

PART ONE – ANN AND E. E.

CHAPTER ONE

Early Years

Music gives a soul to the universe, wings to the imagination and life to everything.
Plato

I reckon that I was quite an unusual sixteen-year-old – even for 1956. I was born into a semi-musical family, in that my father boasted about being tone deaf (a problem which, according to Oliver Sacks in Musicophilia,[1] he may have shared with five per cent of the population), while my mother was the daughter of Albert Cazabon, a professional violinist and composer of light music, who had also for nine years been the conductor of the Sydney Theatre Orchestra. Although she herself went into first Art and then acting before, upon the family's return from Australia, abandoning all that in order to marry and rear a large Catholic family, my mother always had a tremendous love of music, which she passed on to all six of her children. As the eldest, I also had to play a large part in helping with the younger ones. (Besides being tone deaf, my father boasted that he hated children!)

I was rejected at birth for being the wrong sex, and so my childhood was very unhappy. My father had been the eldest son of an eldest son of an eldest son and he (perhaps understandably!) wanted to carry on the family tradition. Also, going to Cambridge University was another Merivale tradition and – since, besides not being beautiful like my mother, I was clearly not 'Oxbridge material' – my father was extremely successful in brainwashing me into believing that I was "no good either at or for anything at all". My only escape was books and music. I learnt to read before I started school, but my family attributed that to tuition from my maiden aunt who was a primary school teacher, rather than to any innate ability that I might have been born with. At the end of my first year of primary school I was kept down. My father said it was because l was stupid, which I naturally believed, but many years later my mother confided to me that she thought it had been because the teachers had found me useful at helping some of the other children in the class to read. It had never occurred to her to go into the school and challenge them on the matter.

I learnt many years later, both from having therapy myself and from my training as a therapist, that children – well, adults too for that matter – often cope with pain by cutting off from it, but this ultimately tells upon health. Absorption in books and music undoubtedly served me well in helping me to cut off from my pain, and both my teacher, Dr Roger Woolger, and the homoeopath/osteopath who has been treating me since 1987, have worked hard at getting me to be more in touch with my feelings. Nowadays I am extremely grateful for the difficulties of my early years because without them I would certainly never have become either a therapist or a writer.

From when I was nine until after I had graduated from Bristol University we lived at number 9 Charlotte Street, a four-storey Georgian terraced house with both a basement and a cellar, situated almost opposite St George's church, a venue now renowned for high quality concerts in Bristol. Since my bedroom was on the top floor, it always seemed to me to be a waste of time to walk up or down the stairs without simultaneously reading a book. Our house was within walking distance of the public library, and so, even though one was only permitted to take out one book at a time, I was rarely without something new to read.

In the early days before my teenage years my only source of music was the wireless. Fortunately my parents had installed Rediffusion, which was a business that distributed radio and TV signals through wired relay networks. I had a speaker and a switch in my bedroom and so I could easily listen to the Third Programme at any time when I wasn't at school, cooking for the family or helping to look after my five younger brothers and sisters. That was another way of escaping temporarily from my father's criticism – especially since he had narrowly survived polio in his youth and his consequent gammy leg was an impediment to climbing all those stairs.

It was my mother who first introduced me to the great composers, and I well remember deciding at the age of about ten or eleven that Haydn and Tchaikovsky were my two favourites. I even have a clear memory of switching on the Third Progamme after something I knew I had heard before had started and saying to myself excitedly, "It's either Haydn or Tchaikovsky!" (Nowadays I admit to occasionally being unsure as to whether a work is by Haydn or Mozart, but how the former could ever be confused with Tchaikovsky I find somewhat baffling. Still, I certainly wasn't more than eleven at the time.)

Soon after I had started secondary school (Clifton High School for Girls – I think I only got in at the second attempt on account of my father's elevated position as Head of the Bristol Royal Infirmary group of hospitals[2]), it was somehow decided that I should have violin lessons. A few of us started together in a group, but for me these lessons were absolute torture because I was *so* bad at it. My maternal grandparents lived in Hampstead, and when I visited them I had to take my violin with me and play it to my grandfather. This was even greater torture than my lessons at school, since the poor man would almost tear out his hair in despair at my lack of proficiency. How well I remember him saying that he simply could not understand how I could love music so much and yet be so bad at "playing the fiddle"! (Fifty-five or more years later I found out the reason to my own complete satisfaction and will recount it later.) However, having grandparents in Hampstead was a great boon during my teenage years because I could stay with them in the summer holidays and treat myself to a few Promenade concerts. And I mostly did promenade, for financial reasons.

By the time I was twelve I had managed to save £5 from my pocket money to buy myself a watch. Two years later I had somehow raised the vast sum of £14 for a Hercules bicycle, and I was thenceforth able to cycle to and from school and also to my friends' houses at weekends. (The main thing that united the six of us was being bad at, and hating, games and gym.)

It must have been around the same time that my family acquired a Pye Black Box (though we actually chose a brown one). This was regarded as an enormous expense, but my father presumably agreed to the purchase because he loved my mother so dearly and appreciated how much being able to play recorded music would mean to her. The thrill was a match for the watch and the bicycle, and now I had something else to save up for.

By this time my taste had extended in a big way to Beethoven. (In those days Friday night at the Proms was always 'Beethoven Night', so I used to make sure that my visits to my grandparents' included a Friday.) The first LP record that I bought was the Pastoral Symphony; it cost £2, so I had to wait many weeks before being able to afford it. Not too long after that, however, I discovered to my great delight that there was a record library in Park Street. My brother John, who is a bit over seven years my junior and by far the most musically gifted member of our family, was by this time completely potty about Mozart. I have vivid memories of walking down the hill with him and having long discussions with Judith, who looked after the library, before walking home with a precious new loan or two clutched under our arms. Only yesterday (Sunday, 9 June 2013) John emailed me ecstatically about having just sung Elgar's 'Ave Maria' and 'Ave Verum Corpus' at mass that morning. Incidentally I am sure that he would *never* have confused Haydn with Tchaikovsky, even at a much more tender age than eleven! His favourite instrument in those days was the French horn, he was ten when Dennis Brain died, and I remember him suddenly becoming so ill when he heard the news that he promptly had to retire to bed. He told me quite recently that he still hadn't really got over that death.

Elgar probably first came into my life only a little bit later than Beethoven. I know for sure that I was sixteen at the time and that I felt as though I had always known him. And when I say "him" I'm talking about the man himself even more than his music. I don't recall searching the library for books about Haydn, Tchaikovsky or Beethoven, but I shall never forget the exciting day when I came across Dora Penny's book[3] in the library. The *Enigma Variations* would certainly have been one of the first of EE's works, if not *the* first, that I fell for, and I read and re-read that book, feeling completely sure that 'Dorabella' was madly in love with him too. Curiously, I was very jealous of her but not at all of Alice Elgar, but again I eventually discovered the reason for that. I no longer recall what other books I read; Michael Kennedy's highly esteemed biography[4] was to be published a whole twelve years later and, though I see from Diana McVeagh's book,[5] which now also graces our shelves, that she had a study of Elgar's life and music published in 1955, I didn't remember her name when we bought *Elgar the Music Maker* from the Birthplace Museum. But at sixteen I certainly read enough to convince me that I would never get over the fact that Elgar had died six years before I was born. Most sixteen-year-old girls these days would of course have a boyfriend and, even in my day, many had crushes on either a film or a pop star, but I was never interested in pop music and in my inner romantic life at that time there was only EE. My brother John now claims, though I find it hard to believe, since I have always had even less talent for drawing than for music, that I did quite a reasonable copy of a portrait of Elgar and stuck it on my bedroom wall.

I also remember in those early days absolutely loving the *Introduction and Allegro* as well as the *Serenade* for Strings, and I certainly heard *Cockaigne*, *Falstaff* and probably the *First*

Symphony on the Third Programme through the Rediffusion speaker in my bedroom. My great love for his violin concerto undoubtedly followed quickly too. In view of what I was to discover much later about my past, it is hardly surprising that this concerto affected me so deeply, for Michael Kennedy describes it as "Elgar's most personal work, a self-communing and a declaration of secret love."

It must have been around that time that my parents decided to give me an allowance rather than just pocket money. From that I was expected to buy all my clothes and so on, but clothes were probably sometimes sacrificed for concert tickets as well as for gramophone records. My parents took me to various concerts at the Colston Hall (I particularly remember hearing Myra Hess with them), but before too very long I was deemed old enough to walk there and back by myself. (I always walked rather than cycled, but maybe that was because my Sturmey Archer 3-speed gear couldn't cope with the steepest section of Park Street. Or perhaps I simply couldn't afford cycle lamps as well as the concert tickets!) At home in my bedroom I spent hours meticulously cutting up all my concert programmes and sticking them onto paper in a big file in alphabetical order of composers. Upon one of my many moves of the ensuing fifty plus years I threw the file out – something I now regret. Apart from the fact that the conductor I saw most frequently was Adrian Boult, I remember little about which works I heard or didn't hear performed live during those years. I would dearly love to see now to what extent my discovery of Elgar was aided by concerts I attended on my own in the Colston Hall.

Although my violin lessons were such an abysmal failure and I was very bad at sight reading, I had a good voice and so was permitted to sing soprano in the school choir. In the sixth form we walked down College Road (normally forbidden territory!) to join forces with Clifton College to perform the *Brahms Requiem*, under the baton of the renowned, one-armed Douglas Fox. We girls were all terrified of Dr Fox, but I was nevertheless absolutely bowled over by the Brahms. I had passed O level music, but only just because, although I was good at the theory, I was hopeless at both the aural and the oral. Nevertheless, when it was time to go up into the sixth form, those in charge decided that I should make an attempt at doing A level music and start piano lessons to help with that. The reason for this was that my five close friends, who were all deemed to be 'Oxbridge material', were going into 6A to do two or three A levels each, and the teachers thought it would not be good for me to be separated from them. I was only considered qualified to do French A level, which meant that strictly I should go into 6B. Only those doing at least two A levels were admitted to 6A, yet even after, for the above-mentioned reason, I had been forced to abandon A level Music at the end of the first term, I was allowed to remain in the same class as my friends. I give the teachers credit for that.

In June 2013, my husband and I joined the West Midlands Branch of the Elgar Society on their annual jaunt, and the next day we visited my school friend Lyn in Wells. When I told her about the jaunt, she said that she always associated Elgar with yoghurt! I had no recollection of this at all, but Lyn assured me that I had discovered both EE and yoghurt at around the same time and had introduced them enthusiastically to my friends more or less simultaneously. Fruit-flavoured yoghurt was not yet available and Lyn, herself a flautist at the time as well as a member of our school choir, told me that she had taken to EE much more readily than to the yoghurt.

Lyn's father was a surgeon in my father's hospital and, when she was celebrating her twelfth birthday and her parents took me with her and our other four friends to see *Swan Lake*, I was suddenly sick during the interval. Lyn's father immediately diagnosed appendicitis and I was rushed off in an ambulance while the others, laughing about my having "eaten too many of the birthday chocolates", enjoyed the rest of the ballet and then went back to her house to spend the night. (Nights away were always a great excitement, which was why I had lied to my mother beforehand that my stomach ache had got better. She had, unbeknown to me, been trying for some years to convince our GP that I had a grumbling appendix, and the pain had always disappeared by the time he arrived at the house!) But for me by far the worst thing about the operation was that, when I was sent home from the hospital the school holidays were just starting and, by the time they were over, I was declared "recovered". So I missed missing games!

I have still never seen the second half of *Swan Lake*, which shows that Tchaikovsky didn't remain among my top favourites. During the many 'black moods' (which is what Helen Weaver called Elgar's) that pervaded my adolescence and early adulthood I would often listen to a Tchaikovsky symphony, but that would accentuate the depression. Gradually I learnt that whenever I needed to be lifted up, some Bach, Beethoven or Mozart was much more effective. I still, however, really like Tchaikovsky's *Serenade for Strings*, even if it isn't quite on a par with the Elgar one.

The only apparent reason for my being good at French was that, at the age of nine when my sister Philippa, who is number five in the family, was on the way, I had been despatched to cousins in France for three months. (My maternal grandmother's sister had married a Frenchman and so the third generation in France were my second cousins.) While staying with my godfather's family in St Germain-en-Laye I went to school for a whole term and, despite being painfully shy, I was soon taken by outsiders to be French. (My children refuse to believe that I have ever been either shy or unassertive but, when as a first year undergraduate I returned to live with the same family while following a course at the Sorbonne, I was always introduced as the cousin who had cried at breakfast because she was too shy to say that she didn't like sugar in her breakfast hot milk. At twenty this did nothing to help me overcome the problem! Again, I needed therapy to deal with my shyness and lack of confidence.)

In the sixth form I was able to study Spanish to O level and took to it like a duck to water. This gave rise to a realisation that I had a natural talent for languages and I was consequently allowed to stay on at school an extra year in order to do A level Spanish, which in turn enabled me to be accepted for Bristol University to study for a joint degree in the two languages. Nowadays I feel sure that I could also have managed A level Latin, but at the time my O level grade was not deemed high enough for that. In fact the only reason I even passed O Level Latin was because the teacher who told the whole set that we were going to fail left one term before the examination. Had I been taught by the teacher who inspired two of my friends to become classicists, I don't doubt that I could have achieved good grades in Latin. Later, when my children were in their teens, I made up partially for this lacuna by taking Italian to A level. (I have not, however, ever liked German, but would you like German if you had been gassed by the Nazis?)

But prior to entering the sixth form I was once again despatched to France, this time for the summer holiday. I stayed with the same family, but in their summer house right on the edge of the Lac d'Annecy. How I loved that place! I took with me some of the literature I was due to be embarking upon in the sixth form and learnt reams of French Romantic poetry by heart. I shall never forget swimming daily in the lake and then gazing at it through Lamartine's eyes while drying myself in the sun. The fact that Lamartine's[6] was actually the Lac du Bourget rather than that of Annecy was immaterial, and my personal, private, equivalent to that poet's 'beloved' was of course Edward Elgar.

I had not, however, taken any records of EE's music with me. Worse still, I soon discovered that, although there was quite a good selection of records in the house, my cousins had never even heard of Elgar! They do nevertheless have to be given credit for introducing me to the Beethoven quartets. I think it was the Opus 74 and the Opus 127 that they had on records and, when I wasn't swimming or learning poetry and dreaming of sailing on the lake with Elgar, I listened to those quartets over and over. After my return home (while still retaining a very soft spot for the Pastoral Symphony[7]) my Beethoven focus soon shifted from his orchestral to his chamber works, and likewise with Haydn, Mozart, Schubert and – a bit later – Brahms. The four sisters in the family were all older than me and, as well as smoking cigarettes, they were beginning to get interested in going out with boys. Since I refused to smoke following the 1954 lung cancer scare and my decision that the easiest solution was never to start, I was accused of being *"une enfant trop sage"*. As for their younger brothers, who were closer to me in age, they scarcely communicated with me at all, which seemed to me to be fairly natural. After all, I thought to myself, why would they be interested in anyone so unattractive as myself? And even if I were attractive, what would be the use since the only man I could ever desire had already been dead for twenty-two years?

At Bristol University our Choral Society sang Haydn's *Creation* and Walton's *Belshazzar's Feast*, which I again greatly enjoyed, but we never sang any Elgar either at school or university. Also, one of the lecturers in the Spanish Department formed a little choir. His wife was Catalan and, besides persuading me to do mediaeval Catalan as my special subject in the third year, he taught us one or two folk songs in that language as well as in Castilian Spanish. I still retain in my head a fairly long and very sad Spanish ballad, which I occasionally pluck up the courage to bring out as my 'party piece', always to considerable acclaim.

By this time my maternal grandparents had left Hampstead and were living in the basement of our house, but fortunately for my grandfather I had now given up the violin as well as my piano lessons, which had been scarcely any more successful.

Another fairly early memory I have is of my mother assuring me that "you will get to like Bach when you're older". I was twenty when I discovered how right she was, and my introduction to Johann Sebastian may well have been hearing the sounds of my grandfather playing the great Chaconne wafting up from the basement. Another of his favourites was the César Franck sonata, but he didn't introduce me to the Elgar violin sonata.

Pam Thonger and I were persuaded when we were accepted at Bristol to be guinea pigs on a new Joint French and Spanish degree course but, when all the French students were sent off to the Sorbonne for the second half of our first year, it was left to our own devices to find Spanish courses to follow in Paris. That proved to be too much of an ordeal on top of our lectures in French and our social life and, when we got into the third year, the French lecturers rarely took on board the fact that the two of us still had Spanish lectures to attend and essays to write for that department. But we both nevertheless graduated with respectable second class degrees[8] (I with a 'Special Mention in Spoken French'). That achievement had, however, no apparent impact on my father. A number of years later, when the whole family were gathered for Christmas and my youngest brother, who was in his final year at Clifton College and thinking about university, had brought home his school report. After reading it out to us all, my father commented, "Well, William, you're the only member of the family who's any good, aren't you?"

After university, not knowing what to do apart from wanting to use my languages without going into school teaching, I did a secretarial course in Bristol before moving to London for my first job. Then, for the next twelve years, I pursued full time an interest that I had acquired as a member of a rather left-wing group within the University Catholic Society: working to help the Third World. This was not yet regarded as normal in those days, and my Conservative father doubtless disapproved of the poorly paid jobs I obtained, but thinking about people whose plight was worse than my own possibly saved me from sinking into clinical depression. In London I joined a University Catholic choir and enjoyed singing with them at mass each Sunday. But we never sang any Elgar there either.

In 1969 my languages and Third World interests combined led me to editorial positions with Church organisations in Geneva. I took with me both a wireless (when was that word changed to 'radio'?) and the tape recorder that I had been given for my 21st birthday. Thanks to the latter, my music collection by then consisted entirely of large tapes filled with works that I had recorded from the Third Programme. In Geneva my salary didn't run to concert tickets and so, apart from my precious tapes, my main source for listening was France Musique, but I don't recall that France Musique ever went in for Elgar. Nor of course did the Geneva madrigal choir that I joined.

In 1972 David Pearson was granted two years' leave of absence from the Mathematics Department of Hull University in order to take up a research post he had been offered at the Département de Physique Théorique in Geneva. When we met we were both getting over big heartbreaks (in my case it was a Spaniard who played me Bach on his guitar and gave me records of Casals playing the *'Cello Suites* for my birthday, but I can't remember whether I had more success in getting him to appreciate Elgar than I did with my Christmas pudding. Quite likely I did!). David and I got to know each other fairly slowly, and as we did we gradually found out that our tastes in music were more or less identical. He knew more about the Beethoven piano sonatas and the Schubert *Lieder* than I did, and was already a bit into Mahler and Bartok, but I knew more of the works of Elgar and Bach than he did. So we broadened each other's horizons somewhat and, since University of Geneva salaries were about twice what David had been earning at Hull, he could afford to buy concert tickets for me as well as for himself. We particularly enjoyed the summer open-air concerts in the Hôtel de Ville, but they never played any Elgar there.

We were married in April 1974, and in the autumn of that year I reluctantly left my beloved Geneva for Hull. But the change of scene was well compensated for by the excitement of starting a family. Gradually, too, David and I added to our precious joint record collection (my tape recorder having now died) and, after Paul was born, we joined a babysitting circle. That enabled us to go to concerts in both Hull and York. I never got round to joining a choir in that area, though, because I knew that I wouldn't be good enough for the Bach choir and, from their advertised programmes, the Hull Choral Union had little appeal to me. In any case, rearing two natural children, adopting a third, and doing voluntary work with organisations such as CAFOD and Christian Aid as well as getting involved in my Catholic parish church activities, was quite enough to keep me fully occupied. So life continued in much the same way for me until my spiritual path began to change during the early 1990s.

Notes

1. *MUSICOPHILIA – Tales of Music and the Brain*, Oliver Sacks, Picador, 2008.
2. Stephen Merivale (1912–1978) was later awarded a CBE for his services to the National Health Service, in the foundation of which he had played a large part. I suspect that he is now turning in his grave at the present state of the NHS! (Our house in Charlotte Street was the property of the Bristol Royal Infirmary.) He was also the first hospital administrator to introduce flexible visiting hours – a practice which in due course spread to other hospitals in the country.
3. *EDWARD ELGAR – Memories of a Variation* by Mrs. Richard Powell, Oxford University Press, 1937.
4. *PORTRAIT OF ELGAR*, Michael Kennedy, Oxford University Press, 1968.

5. *ELGAR – The Music Maker*, Diana McVeagh, The Boydell Press, 2007.

6. *Le Lac* is probably the best known of this celebrated French Romantic's poems. In it Lamartine writes nostalgically about sailing on an Alpine lake with his now lost beloved.

7. In his biography *A Portrait of Elgar*, Michael Kennedy tells of the composer's delight at buying the score of this symphony and taking it down to the riverside to study!

8. Our experimental course was subsequently changed from a three- to a four-year one.

CHAPTER TWO

New Spiritual Paths

There's one thing worse than writing and that's not writing.
The novelist Andrew Martin talking to Sarah Walker on
Radio 3 on 9 January 2013.

When I first arrived back from Geneva, David's colleagues told
me that we wouldn't be in the Hull area very long because he
would be sure to get a Chair somewhere. They were in due
course proved right about his promotion, but it was to a Personal
Chair at Hull and so, apart from a couple of house moves, we
stayed put for the next thirty years. I missed the mountains, but
fortunately David was frequently invited back to Geneva to work
during the summer vacation. He found the atmosphere there
very stimulating for his research, and it was also lovely for me to
be there without having to go to work during the week. The
children too all became enamoured of the open-air pools and
parks and are still very fond of the city. Once Paul was old
enough to take charge of the younger two, and even more after
we had become what the Americans call "empty nesters", we
could again enjoy the summer concerts in the Hôtel de Ville and
the church of St Germain (though still no Elgar of course!).

After we had adopted Christopher in November 1979 my life
became more full than ever. He is half Sierra Leonean and before
long David and I both got deeply involved in anti-racist activities. I was also active in my local Catholic parish and with the
Church Justice and Peace movement. Later too, when the
children were preparing successively to go off to university, I did
little bits of French and Spanish teaching to supplement the
family income. Music was never absent during these busy years,
however, and our main concert-going was to the Hull University

Chamber Music Society and the Yorkshire Bach Choir's performances in York under Peter Seymour. Our record collection gradually changed to CDs, and of course Elgar was as ever in the forefront, even though I *had* long since come to terms with the fact of his having lived "too soon for me".

Then, in 1987, my mother died of cancer at only seventy-five and, while looking after her in Oxford right at the end of her life, I met my sister Philippa's 'alternative practitioner', who was also treating my mother. From this I learnt that he regarded my mother as a "typical cancer victim" whose life he could possibly have saved if he had caught her earlier, and this gave rise for me to a new perspective on questions of health. At my request Philippa's Oxford practitioner recommended a fellow osteopath, who was also a homoeopath, in North Yorkshire (somewhat nearer to Hull than Oxford). As I mentioned before, he is still treating me all these years later, and in fact I now periodically practise my own therapy in his clinic. Inspired by the success for our whole family of homoeopathic treatment, I enrolled for an Adult Education course in Hull in Alternative Medicine. This caused me to make new friendships as well as find new interests but, again as I mentioned in the Introduction, my Catholicism was for a while a stumbling block when it came to the question of reincarnation, in which many of the friends I now had believed.

In 1991 a lecture that I heard in Hull on Edgar Cayce changed all that. Learning that Cayce, who cured people all over the world by giving both medical and 'past life' readings, had been a devout Christian all his life made me really prick up my ears, and I promptly joined the Edgar Cayce Association and devoured a number of books on him and on related subjects. At the Association's conference in 1992 I met various people who had been greatly helped by receiving 'past life readings'. Cayce himself died in 1945, but someone recommended to me Aron Abrahamsen, an American clairvoyant, again a Christian, who had worked with Cayce. Wanting to know both why I had chosen my father prior to incarnating this time round (a thing I found extremely difficult to believe) and why we were having so many difficulties with our adopted son, I sent off for a reading from Abrahamsen.

This reading arrived in July 1992, and the following month we were due to go to Spain for a family holiday. Abrahamsen told me in the reading about five past lives which were relevant to my present one, and they all shed light on my closest relationships in this life. But also, to my utter astonishment, he said that I had "come this time partly as a writer – to disseminate information on the spiritual life". Well although, partly thanks to my editorial career, my writing abilities had improved since I had finished with full time education, and although I had occasionally had letters on racism published in newspapers, I had never for a single moment had any serious writing aspirations. However, one of my past lives that Abrahamsen had described was as a nun in Spain and, on our travels the following month, we stopped one evening for a picnic in a little Spanish square outside a large church that was attached to a monastery or convent. Gazing at the high wall opposite us set me off musing about what living a secluded life behind such a wall would be like, and this musing somehow gave me the idea for my first book – a book that would demonstrate how my previous lives had influenced my present one. I thought about it throughout the holiday and started writing as soon as we were home again.

At that point I found it completely impossible to imagine myself ever getting a book published, but my sister Philippa had recently made the acquaintance of Edwin Courtenay, a young English clairvoyant in Yorkshire, and we went to see him together. He assured me that my book would be published, and he supplemented this assertion with information about other past lives which he saw as relevant to what was gradually becoming apparent as my "life's work". Around that time too I went with

Cynthia, a friend from my parish, to see a clairvoyant in Hull, and she saw me publishing "numbers of books". This I *absolutely* could not believe but, including my not-yet-quite-finished book on Adoption, this little book is my sixth and I at present have ideas in my head for a further three.

Cynthia (who now calls herself Thia) and I had only found out gradually that we had similar spiritual interests. We lent each other books, and it was she who first introduced me to Sai Baba. She had been having a crisis of faith when she prayed to Jesus to show her the way and, on her next visit to the local library, two books about Sai Baba had almost fallen off the shelf on to her head. One of them was *A Catholic Priest meets Sai Baba* by Mario Mazzoleni, and it was this one that convinced me too that following him need not conflict with my religion. For Sathya Sai Baba came not to found a new religion but to unite them all. He always encouraged Hindus to be "better Hindus", Buddhists to be "better Buddhists", Christians "better Christians" and so on. Nowadays, even following his demise on Easter Sunday 2011, people from all over the world and of all religions flock to his ashram in their thousands, and the numbers even of Muslims who visit are increasing all the time. There are still daily lectures at the ashram as well as devotional singing, all the major religious festivals are celebrated there, and just after Christmas a multi-faith service is led by Father Charles Ogada, a Nigerian Catholic priest.

So I wanted to remain in the Church of my upbringing, but it was in due course my local parish church that rejected *me*. Thia founded a Hull Sai Baba group with my support, and she advertised it by putting up notices in her window (which happened to be in the same street as the church). Once wind was got of my allegiance to "this Indian guru", I was banned from reading the epistle at mass as well as from being a Eucharistic minister.

However, my spiritual interests had already taken me beyond the Church of my upbringing: partly because of its present-day non-acceptance of reincarnation, partly because (unlike, for instance, Buddhism) it teaches nothing about the afterlife even though that is purported to be so central to its creed. Whenever I comment on this latter point to Christians who are not Sai Baba devotees, their response is always, "But we *cannot* know anything about what lies beyond the grave... It's all a mystery..." But I have never liked mysteries and my many years of reading and research have revealed to me a great deal of information, which, now that I am on the 'last lap', I regard as very useful. When I find many people who do not know each other, or who have not read each other's books, recounting extraordinarily similar experiences from such things as near-death-experiences (commonly referred to as NDEs), that is for me sufficient 'proof' of the evidence. I conveyed a lot of this information in my third book,[1] to which I appended a bibliography.[2] The letters that Helen 'wrote' to EE after passing into spirit are fuelled by the extensive research that I have done into this subject.

Also, in Deep Memory Process therapy we do a lot of work after the client has gone through a death into what is known as the *Bardo*. This Tibetan word literally means 'between islands', and it is in this state that much of the healing can take place. For looking back on a life with the aid (normally) of spirit guides, guardian angels or Masters enables people to see what its purpose had been, what they had learnt or failed to learn, and – most important of all – to forgive themselves. In the *Bardo* too one can meet up with lost loved ones, friends or enemies, and "have it out" with the latter in order to make peace. Again, people's experiences in regression bear so many similarities that I find it impossible not to believe that they are universal.

It was only after I had been writing for a while about my own past lives that I thought of training as a past life regression therapist. I then attended an introductory weekend workshop that Dr Roger Woolger gave in London and was completely enthralled. Roger, however, sent me off to do some 'body work' before he would train me, giving as his reason that I was "too much in my head". In the form of therapy that he developed the body is key because, as Roger always explained so well in his teaching, traumatic memories are passed on to new bodies in new incarnations and stored there without our being consciously aware of it. (For this we use the Sanskrit word *samskaras*.) As I mentioned in the Introduction, unlike most schools of past life regression therapy, Woolger did not use hypnotherapy, which he said tended to make for dissociation, while he found being "completely *in* the past life" to be more effective than just observing it. And for people who have coped with pain by cutting off from it, getting in touch with the body tends to be more difficult.

So I duly went to the person he recommended for the body work, but also enrolled for a course with the London College of Past Life Regression Studies. This was because, despite having by now had a great deal of therapy, I had yet completely to get over my father's brain washing and so imagined that I would never be "good enough" to train with the man who was regarded as the world expert in the field. I found the London course very useful for the theory but, since those weekends of study, sitting on uncomfortable chairs in Regent's College, had not given much opportunity for practice, I lacked confidence for getting started even after obtaining my diploma. I did start up tentatively working in Hull, with some success, but soon decided that being precluded from obtaining a Woolger diploma need not prevent me from attending one of his full week training workshops.

This proved to be addictive and, after my fifth (or was it sixth?) Woolger workshop, and presenting a case study at a graduate weekend, Roger presented me with his diploma in DMP. During this training I also worked on my own at home with John Bradshaw's exercises for "healing the inner child", and all this combined enabled me finally to release those feelings of being "no good". It was only some years after my father's death that I got over my fear of him, and of the resulting fear of men in general that any psychotherapist would expect in someone with my upbringing. From Woolger workshops I found out that my father, whose own unfortunate attitude to girls had stemmed at least in part from my overbearing grandmother and his no doubt difficult childhood, had been reinforcing 'complexes' that I had brought in with me. I was thus able both to make peace with him, and with my mother who had never been able to defend me against him, and to appreciate that there had been good reasons for my early difficulties. Rather than fear, I now feel sorry for him for having been unable to appreciate the joys brought by either young children or music! And nowadays my previous unhappiness is no more than a memory that affects the excellent life I have at present in no way at all; it is as though I were now in a completely new and much more worthwhile incarnation.

The most dramatically effective regression that I ever did, however, was towards the end of 2006, after I had been qualified as a DMP practitioner for well over five years. Roger summoned all his graduates to a week's refresher workshop, and I took with me an issue that had been troubling me virtually all my life: an intense fear of travel. (People who knew me laughed at this because we have always travelled so much, but I assure you that it was very real.) David and I had decided to make a lengthy trip to India early in 2007. I was due to spend three weeks at Sai Baba's ashram in the January, and so we agreed that David would join me there for the last week and that we would then travel around on our own together for seven weeks, making plans as we went along. It was exciting because there was so much of that amazing country that we wanted to see, but I was at the same time incredibly nervous about it.

For the practice that always interspersed Roger's lectures at his workshops I paired up with my good friend François, who is an extremely experienced counsellor and therapist and in whose hands I felt completely safe and at ease. After I had told him about the problem that I wanted to look at, François took me into a life in which I was a very young, probably Native American, boy who was fleeing with his family and other tribespeople from some white men. The following account is in the first person, that being the normal practice in regression. Because everyone was in a hurry and my legs were shorter than the rest of my family's, I very soon got left behind. By the time that night had begun to fall I was completely lost, and also terrified by the sounds being made all around me by wild animals. When François asked me, "What happens next? Do you get attacked by one of these animals?" I was completely unable to answer his questions; I simply couldn't see what happened next. So this is an example of where the Woolger 'body work' can be used to great effect. François then 'attacked' me physically, making growling noises and so on, and my body, which had recorded the memory even though my mind had not, reacted violently and uncontrollably, just as though I was really being attacked by a bear. While I was sitting up, retching, Roger happened to walk past. I can still hear his voice exclaiming, "Someone's got *Ann* into her body!" After my (the little boy's) death, I saw the brown bear who had caused it very clearly and, with François' assistance, the bear and I had a literal 'bear hug' and made friends. (In such circumstances we make good use of pillows rather than recruiting a real bear!) Following this, most powerful, regression, I went off to India without any fear at all and, apart from the inevitable frustrations and difficulties that will always beset people travelling on their own in that continent, the whole trip was most successful.

During the two plus years of my Woolger training, Jen, one of my fellow students, who had a large house in Dorset, kindly volunteered her abode for practising the therapy on each other. These weekends were supervised by Roger's then deputy for England. (Roger, though English, lived mainly in America.) It is said to be advisable for therapists to have undergone at least 200 hours of therapy themselves, and of course mutual support is always invaluable as well. So in 2001, Kris, who had like me just graduated with the Woolger diploma, and who ran a guest house in France called Le Moulin, suggested that we all meet there for a week. For two successive years Roger's deputy came with us to Le Moulin as a practice supervisor, but as we gradually became more experienced in the work we felt we no longer needed either supervision or an agenda. Le Moulin was in due course sold, but we were reluctant to abandon either our annual reunions or the name of 'Mouliners', and now we are fortunately able to rent a nearby *gîte* owned by Kris' brother. This is an important point because it was at one of these *Mouliners'* meetings that Helen Weaver unexpectedly raised her head. First, however, I will recount how Elgar came back into my life more forcibly than ever.

Notes

1. *DISCOVERING THE LIFE PLAN – Eleven Steps to Your Destiny*, Ann Merivale, O-BOOKS, 2012.
2. Since this was published, another strongly evidential book has come out, which I would recommend even (or particularly!) to the most sceptical. It is written by a distinguished American neuro-surgeon by name of Eben Alexander and is entitled *PROOF OF HEAVEN: A Nuero-surgeon's Journey into the Afterlife.*

CHAPTER THREE

Move to the West Midlands and the 'BIG DISCOVERY'

Every age has a secret society of congenial spirits. Draw the circle tighter you who belong to one another; that the truth of art may shine ever more clearly, spreading joy and blessings everywhere.
Robert Schumann

David's retirement in 2004 left us free to move to a part of the country that we found more attractive. We had already fallen in love with Shropshire, and a June evening walk along the Teme caused us to settle quickly on Ludlow. (Michael Kennedy quotes a letter written in October 1933 by Elgar to Florence Norbury from the South Bank Nursing Home: "I lie here hour after hour, thinking of our beloved Teme – surely the most beautiful river that ever was and it belongs to you too – I love it more than any other"!) Only after we had made the move, however, did we begin to discover all the advantages of living in Ludlow. I had thought that we would miss York for music. Ha ha! (Well, I do still plan to go back one year for the York Early Music Festival, and we would of course love to hear the Yorkshire Bach Choir again.) Virtually all my life I had read so much about the Three Choirs Festival, yet it was only after we had arrived here that I suddenly realised how accessible all three of the venues now were to us, so that Festival is now an important part of our annual calendar; Malvern, which has numerous excellent concerts throughout the year, is only an hour's drive away, even the Birmingham Symphony Hall is accessible thanks to coach transport organised by LUDTAG (the Ludlow Theatre and Arts Group), and in Ludlow itself there is a music society that puts on five excellent chamber concerts a year.

In addition to all that, I soon joined the Ludlow Choral Society, under the baton of Patrick Larley, who is a delight to sing with. He works us quite hard, but always with an almost Elgarian sense of humour. (That is of course Elgar in his *good* moods!) A composer himself as well as a gifted all round musician, Patrick may for all I know be a better conductor than Elgar, since the latter was never greatly reputed for conducting anything other than his own works. He has also to some extent opened my mind to composers that I would have previously dismissed as too modern for my taste (for instance, Cecilia McDowall). At the moment, while I'm putting the finishing touches to this manuscript, our choir are rehearsing for the 2013 Christmas concert and learning Patrick's delightful setting of Robert Herrick's poem 'Ceremonies'. Herrick, who was born in 1591, became a disciple of Ben Johnson and took holy orders in 1623, wrote at a time when mince pies still contained real meat as well as dried fruit and spices! Patrick's music, however, which has a very effective church bell accompaniment, is hardly seventeenth century in style. And in his composition, *In Praise of Music*, commissioned for the 150th anniversary of the Choral Society, he even has a really lovely melody to the words, "Angel voices ever singing round thy throne of light..." (I say "even" because, in my humble opinion, modern British music is not noted for beautiful tunes!) I mustn't omit either to mention too our brilliant accompanist, Steve Dunachie, also a composer, and who was in addition previously employed by my own university.

Not very long after I had joined the Society, we sang two Elgar songs ('As Torrents in Summer' and 'My Love dwelt in a Northern Land'), which of course delighted me. Then another year – wonder of wonders – we did *The Music Makers*, which was a huge revelation to me. I would in due course have discovered it anyway from the Three Choirs Festival, but am grateful to Patrick for revealing it to me earlier. Maybe the Third Programme and Radio 3 did broadcast it during one of my many absences from the country, but hearing it on Radio 3 or a CD, or even with the wonderful Sarah Connolly in Hereford, cannot quite equal actually singing in it! My favourite bit of this work will always be, "But we, with our dreaming and singing..." *How* is it that Elgar manages to make just a very few notes so powerful that they penetrate instantly right into the depths of one's soul?

But of course one of the very biggest advantages of living in Ludlow is that it only takes me fifty minutes to drive from our house to the Elgar Birthplace Museum. Besides my lamentable ignorance of *The Music Makers*, I didn't discover Elgar's chamber music until after we had moved here. I can immediately hear members of the Elgar Society crying, "Shame on you!", but I've made up for it thanks to the Birthplace Museum's excellent shop, and anyway it's always nice to leave a few wonderful discoveries until late in life.

I first became aware of the existence of the Elgar Society upon our first visit to the Museum, but at that time we were too busy to think of joining it. However, I also had the curious feeling that my love for EE was so deeply personal that it wasn't something that I would be able to share with others. Yet despite that, I eventually changed my mind in July 2010, when David's widowed brother came to stay and expressed a desire to visit the Birthplace for the first time. He generously paid the entrance fee for the three of us, and then I noticed that membership of the Society would entitle us to free admission there for evermore. So we thereupon decided to join the West Midlands branch and have, needless to say, been enormously grateful ever since for the fascinating meetings we have been able to attend, as well as the journals and the excellent company.

At the 2011 Three Choirs Festival in Worcester, we had the interesting experience during the Elgar Society lunch of sitting at the same table as Michael Butterfield, a former music teacher, who was then the Chairman of the Society's South West branch. I naturally started up a conversation about Bristol with him and, when I told him where my family had lived, he exclaimed "Merivale!" It turned out that he had been friends with my brother John when they were both at Clifton Preparatory School, and he told me that it had been hearing the Strauss Horn concertos in our house that had made him decide to take up that instrument. I well remembered my mother having bought that record, but was no doubt buried in French and Spanish homework in my top-floor bedroom while my young brother and his friend were listening to music together a whole two floors below. It was fun to renew the connection because John lost touch with Michael when it was time for them both to move to secondary school and John was sent off to board at The Oratory. (My father, though an Anglican himself, scrupulously kept his promise to have us all brought up Catholic.)

One day after we had joined the Elgar Society I suddenly remembered about Dora Penny's book and determined to re-read it. An internet search revealed it to be long out of print, but I quickly secured an old library copy (not incidentally the Bristol library!) from Amazon (which, as a writer, I normally abhor, but have to admit that it does have its uses). Reading it fifty plus years on, I saw their relationship in a rather different light. The adolescent Ann had obviously been transferring her own love-smittenness (to coin a horrible word!) to 'Dorabella' (Elgar's nickname for her, taken from Mozart's opera *Così fan Tutte).* She had when they first made friends clearly been no more than a youngster who thoroughly enjoyed EE's company, and he hers!

But now to return to my very first visit to the Elgar Birthplace Museum. It was a beautiful day and, when we first went out of the cottage into the lovely garden, I was listening on the headphones provided to Janet Baker singing *Where Corals Lie* from the *Sea Pictures.* This work was again new to me and I found it intensely moving, but the moment we got our first glimpse of the garden, I burst into tears. I have never been a person who weeps easily (I shall never forget Roger Woolger applauding at the first of his workshops during which I cried when being regressed!), and so I found myself a bit taken aback by this unusual reaction. Roger, who always used to start each of his training days with a piece of music and some poetry readings, shared my passions for both Bach and Elgar, and so the next time we met, which was at a meeting of the International Deep Memory Association, I told him about my experience at the Birthplace. His response was, "Well, maybe Elgar's spirit is hanging around the place." I thought that he was quite likely right, but at the same time I felt deep inside that there was something more to it than that.

The garden of the cottage in Lower Broadheath, near Worcester, where Elgar was born.

The question then went on hanging around at the back of my mind until 2012 (several months after Roger's death from cancer. In the meantime I had bought a copy of *The Dream of Gerontius* (with Janet Baker as the angel of course!) from the Birthplace and sent it to him in the hospice). I got out our own identical CD in the spring of that year, when David and I were about to go over

The author sitting with Jemma Pearson's statue of Elgar, which has been placed at the bottom of the garden.

to Bishops Castle for a meeting of their 'Quest' group. The meeting that evening was to be led by Joan Baker, a Shropshire artist of whose work we are both very fond, and who is also reputed in the area for leading meditations. We were each asked to bring along something such as a poem or a piece of music, which had moved us deeply, or even been a turning point in our spiritual life. For me of course it had to be Gerontius' angel at the point after his death and meeting with God, when his soul is being transported to its next port of call, and after that interesting evening in Bishops Castle those wonderful strains kept on and on haunting me as never before.

Then in May, very shortly afterwards, our '*Mouliners*' annual reunion came round, and I took the same CD off with me to France. This was because I now felt an overwhelming desire to find out the reason for what I could only regard as my rather extraordinary emotional attachment to EE. I had with my (according to Roger Woolger over-analytical!) mind tried for a long time to find a reason for my feelings, and had worked out – completely logically – that I couldn't *possibly* have known him personally during his lifetime as Edward Elgar. When my turn for working came round, I began by explaining my question to my friends, mentioning at the same time my 'left-brain' conclusions about having been "elsewhere"[2] during his time on Earth. But my colleagues are long since sufficiently well trained to ignore left-brain conclusions, and Kris put the CD on again on the track that I had already played them, asking whether I could visualise myself listening to it on my deathbed.

Although it is possible to regress oneself (some people being better at it than others), there is something about group energy that invariably makes this work infinitely more effective and powerful. Even more so when it comes to the 'body stuff' that I have mentioned before. As I drifted into an altered state with Janet Baker's voice in the background, seeing in my mind's eye a sick woman lying in bed and about to be transported to another plane, I suddenly started coughing uncontrollably. Then the "ever rational Ann" chipped in with her left-brain and, with her friends' prompting, started reeling off all the names of the principal women in EE's life. As soon as the name Helen Weaver passed my lips *something* happened. It's impossible to explain even to myself, let alone to any sceptic, but my colleagues' immediate certainty that she was the person whose lifetime I had accessed gradually transferred itself to me, if at first reluctantly. So I can only again beg you to take on board the Little Prince's assertion that what is essential is invisible to the eyes. Once that identity had been established, it was then easy for my experienced friends to take me right through all the key points in Helen's life.

Roger Woolger always stressed in his training workshops that "the *body* remembers even when the 'soul' or mind does not", and it was his frequent use of bodily symptoms or feelings as a lead in to a significant past life that distinguished his methods from those of many others in the field. So, when my chest had started becoming increasingly uncomfortable, my colleagues felt that TB (then known as consumption) was a likely cause. But don't worry: I didn't have to stay in that uncomfortable state for the rest of our wonderful week together! DMP therapists are as expert at getting one out of the discomfort as into it; I only needed to remain 'afflicted' while the story was becoming clear. And *how* clear did it become! The period before I as Helen became ill, when the closeness with EE was developing, the violin playing and studies, the departure for New Zealand and marriage in that country to a "safe, well-to-do man" ... all appeared in my head in vivid pictures. Here I will mention that I happen to be a very visual person, but that that is by no means essential for regression because feelings are by far the most important thing when it comes to healing. Roger Woolger always said that he himself was not visual at all and that when he was regressed he only got sounds, smells and so on as well as feelings and emotions.

And an interesting point about this regression is that I hadn't previously known anything at all about Helen's marriage. I later found what I had seen confirmed in Cora Weaver's book that I am about to mention again. Strongest of all the things that I felt were firstly a deep conviction that the drums in the thirteenth Enigma Variation did indeed represent the engines of Helen's ship sailing away from England, and secondly that she had *never* ceased loving him for a single second.

After my return home I inevitably carried on mulling over what had happened in France, but I was at the time busy finishing a little book on soul rescue work[3] as well as being engaged with a much longer project for a broad-based book on adoption. I had for long had in mind to write a sort of sequel to my first book, and so I decided that the life as Helen Weaver would be the start of a book, which I would entitle *A LIFE WITHOUT ELGAR and Other Tales of a Journeying Soul.* I Googled

Helen Weaver without a great deal of success (Facebook mentioned a newspaper article about her written by someone in New Zealand, but the author failed to reply to the message I sent him), and so she simply went on sitting in the back of my mind.

Then in early September we were in Malvern Priory, when I noticed a booklet about it written by one Cora Weaver. The name naturally caught my attention and so I bought a copy. I then soon saw not only that the author was connected to the Weaver family by marriage, but that she had also written a little book about Helen. So I promptly went back to Amazon, and also ABE Books, but on this occasion without success. However, Blackwell's Rare Books kindly replied to an email I sent them, drawing my attention to a copy that was for sale on e-bay. Well, I had never yet used e-bay and felt distinctly nervous about it, but needs must! The initial price seemed pretty reasonable – £11 or so – and I bravely put in a bid for a little bit more.

Then we went off to the Cotswolds on a week's family holiday, but luckily our son Paul had his laptop with him. As the week drew to a close, my family were all concerned about the result of a biopsy I had just had of a lump in my breast, which we were due to obtain from Hereford Hospital on our way home, but I was *much* more concerned about whether or not I was going to secure Cora Weaver's book! Well, although at the very last minute my bid was forced up to nearly £30, which is a great deal of money for such a small book, my luck held. And the book arrived on the morning of the very day on which I had to return to the hospital in order to be prepared for a small (incidentally totally successful) breast cancer operation. So all the hanging around in the hospital in between the different things that had to be done to me was as nothing while I had this exciting little book to read and even more to reflect upon. And every visit to the Macmillan Renton Unit of Hereford hospital involves walking past a large photograph of Elgar that hangs on the wall of one of the corridors!

Now I shall leap forward to the following May (2013). On the 18th of that month, Timothy Day in Hereford (a member of our West Midlands branch of the Elgar Society) held a meeting in his abode, which is the ground floor of Plas Gwyn, where the Elgar family lived from 1904–11. In the very study in which EE had written some of his greatest works, such as the Introduction and Allegro for Strings, The Kingdom, the First Symphony and the Violin Concerto, the composer Anthony Powers gave an interesting talk about Elgar's influence on his work, and this was followed by an equally interesting discussion. This was the second time that David and I had been to a meeting in Plas Gwyn, the first time having been on a horrendously wet day the previous November. Although the previous visit had naturally given me a great thrill, somehow this second one affected me even more strongly. The first time it might have been the worry of driving to Hereford through such awful rain and looking for the house and somewhere to park, or it might have been the fact of making my first longish drive following the cancer operation, that had a slightly adverse effect on me. (David lost his driving licence at seventy on account of eye problems.) However, I prefer to think that the reason this second visit affected me even more powerfully was that on this occasion Elgar's spirit got into communication with me.

Here let me bring up an important question of terminology. At the meeting on May 18th there was talk of the presence of "Elgar's ghost" in his beautiful Plas Gwyn study. Well, in the spiritual work in which I am involved, the term 'ghost' denotes a spirit that has been trapped upon the Earth's plane after death,[4] either because the soul concerned simply doesn't realise that he or she has died, or because he or she doesn't know where to go next. For souls who are "happily dead", and consequently free to travel wheresoever they will, we use the word 'spirit'.

After enjoying a delicious tea, combined with pleasant conversation, in Plas Gwyn, David and I returned home, thankful that the forecast rain for that day had not materialised. I then set about cooking an evening meal and, while I was doing this, some letters between Helen W and EE started busily writing themselves in my head. Normally these days I do all my writing straight onto my desktop PC, but on this occasion I was due to travel the next day to North Yorkshire for a visit to my homoeopath, and the letters didn't seem to want to wait. So I took paper with me as well as a pen and wrote non-stop throughout the train journeys both ways.

Photo no. 3: Elgar's study in Plas Gwyn.

The following week was taken up with preparations for flying to Toulouse for the next *'Mouliners'* meeting, which left me no time for the computer apart from checking my emails, but the letters were still coming through so fast that I carried on writing in longhand on the trains to Bristol as well as on the flight from Bristol. We had a wonderful week as always, but the weather this time was unprecedentedly dreadful for the time of year in southern France, and so during the breaks, instead of swimming

Photo no. 4: The outside of Plas Gwyn.

in the pool as usual or lazing around in the sun, I simply carried on writing in longhand. Never before has anything that I've written come so fast and furiously, and I couldn't help feeling that it was EE himself who was egging me on! I hadn't been writing for very long before I decided that, instead of the normal way in which I write up past lives, HW and EE's relationship could be recounted entirely through letters. So I do hope you will enjoy them!

Notes

1. A CD recording was made of this concert, which also included Vivaldi's *Gloria.* For more information see www.patricklarley.com
2. Even people with the most scientific minds accept that time doesn't really exist, so in DMP we are taught not to expect

past lifetimes all to take place chronologically. Besides, people such as the well-known Dr Michael Newton, the past life regression therapist and writer whom I mentioned in a previous footnote, have given good evidence for people sometimes having parallel lives.

3. *DELAYED DEPARTURE – A Beginner's Guide to Soul Rescue*, O-BOOKS, 2013.

4. In the above-mentioned book, I have explained in some detail how to help such 'ghosts' to move on to a higher plane.

PART TWO

E. E. AND HELEN WEAVER

Imagined Correspondence

30 October 1885

Dearest Ted,

I don't think I'll ever put this letter into the post – I don't think it would be right to do so – but firstly I know that I need to write it purely for my own sake, and secondly I hope, I *really* hope, that somehow or other what I am about to try to put into words will reach you. I needed to sever contact with you for both our sakes: you need to be free to find a woman who is healthier and stronger than I am, someone better equipped to love and support you – the latter perhaps even materially; I need to embark upon a new life for myself on the other side of the globe, in a country whose climate will, I trust, be more beneficial to my failing health. No one can possibly hazard a guess as to how much longer I am likely to live, but of this I am sure: however much grief my departure is at present causing you, that grief would have been greater still if we had married and you had then lost me within no more than a few years.

Ted, my mind is in turmoil and thus it has been for longer than I care to think. Above all, I want you to be eternally sure – as sure as I am myself – that I have *never* not loved you: that our love is and will always be the most precious thing in my life. You may never forget me. May I say that a big bit of me even *hopes* that you will never forget me?! But I trust that one day – preferably sooner rather than later – you will come to appreciate that I, your beloved and loving Nellie, am not the person best suited to your needs. Love, however and deep and true it may be, is one thing; sharing an entire life together is quite another.

I like to imagine you now, at this moment, standing on the shore, staring into the distance at this ship as it slowly shrinks before your eyes, until it finally disappears from your sight altogether. At the same time I like to imagine your heartfelt grief gradually transmuting itself into one of the most beautiful tunes that you have ever written. Let us call it 'catharsis'. Just think of Beethoven, deaf as a post and profoundly traumatised by his failure to hear the amazing sounds that he has just been hammering out on his piano, suddenly putting onto paper the most wonderful string quartet ever composed. A quartet that exceeds in beauty and profundity even those of his revered Haydn and Mozart, a quartet that is *at least* fifty years ahead of his time. That is catharsis: from the depths of despair emerges a precious jewel that will shine brightly for all eternity. And so now I want to imagine *you*, having just plucked from the air, or from one of your beloved trees, a tune that really *speaks* to you, enlarging upon it, then building from it a work that the world will recognise as truly great. A work that will make you famous.

Yes, Ted, you may well now accuse me of "letting my imagination work overtime", but herein lies my dilemma. Much though I would like to think of you standing on the shore as my ship sails away, blowing me an accepting farewell kiss, I know full well that that is not the case. That in fact you are more likely at home in Worcester, in one of your 'black moods', trying to blot me and your sorrows out of your mind. Trying desperately to overcome your grief either by searching out more pupils from whom to earn a pittance, or by scribbling more little snippets of music here and there in the hope of *one* day putting them together into something saleable. Or are you perchance not even *attempting* to overcome your grief, but instead channelling it into walking one of your favourite routes, or even taking a boat ride on the Severn – a repeat of the one we took on our very first date?

Thinking of your grief pains me more than I can say, and I beg you, please, please not to think that I don't share it. How can I ever explain to you what I have been feeling, the torments and the conflicts that I have been going through in recent months?

Breaking off our engagement was the hardest thing I have ever done, and I hope that you have never thought, even for a second, that I did it lightly. I can hear you saying, "But we were so happy together..." and, of course, you're right, we had so many blissfully happy moments. Moments when our violins were in tune with each other and in harmony with our souls; moments when we shared the beauty of those Malvern hills surrounding us, the song of a bird, the smell of a pink rose. But can you not understand too the agonies that I went through when you were in one of your 'black moods'? When your despair at ever achieving what you needed to achieve was so great that there was absolutely nothing I could do to pull you out of it, to give you faith in your abilities, to convince you that our love mattered more than anything else on Earth? Yes, of course, the 'highs' were the pinnacle of ecstasy, but the 'lows' were a deep pit out of which I found it impossible to crawl. And then how could I withstand all that pressure from outside – from my family, from friends and neighbours? "He's only the impoverished son of a piano tuner.... He has so little education... He aspires to be a great musician, but how can you learn music in nothing other than a music shop? And what's more – he's a Roman Catholic! How could a Roman Catholic ever get anywhere in life? You'd never be able to afford to rear a family. If indeed you were capable of rearing a family with your weak lungs and ever-failing health."

Then, Teddy darling, on top of all that, can you even begin to understand what I went through when I had to curtail my violin studies in Leipzig in order to come home and nurse my dear stepmother not so long after my father had died? You visited me in Leipzig. You know just how much it meant to me to be walking the very streets – the hallowed streets – that Johann Sebastian had trod. The city where the GREAT MAN had ended his days. The city whose very stones still ring out with those exquisite cantatas, those amazing Passions, the sublime B Minor Mass, the concerti written for *our* instrument. Our instrument: will I ever play it again? Had we stayed together we could no doubt have encouraged each other in the study of it, but I have less natural talent than you have. I really needed a great teacher such as those of the Leipzig Conservatoire to develop my abilities. Maybe I should have returned there, but somehow it no longer felt right. Then, when my good friend Edith suggested I join her in Bradford and do some teaching there, it seemed to be a good opportunity to earn some much needed money. I needed a break from you as well, and a chance to reflect deeply upon the nature of our relationship. And even if I had managed to complete my studies, would I ever have been able to make a successful career as a violinist? I don't need to tell *you* how difficult it is to make one's mark in this field. How much competition there is. How can I know whether even *you* will gain the recognition you deserve? I can teach of course, but you might have wanted us to have children, which would obviously be time consuming. Would we have been destined for a life as 'church mice', as the saying goes? Love may well be able to keep two souls together, but we have two bodies to keep together as well!

Besides, can I ever make you understand how my stepmother's last months affected me? Ann, your dear mother, still loves and supports you in every way she can, but I lost my mother when I was only thirteen, which seems a long time ago now and my memories of her are fading. My father's second wife filled that gap for me and, as you know, we became very close. It was me she wanted – me she *needed* more than anyone else – to care for her right up to the end. So care for her I did to the very best of my abilities, but it wasn't easy. Not only was I continually grief-stricken at the thought of losing her, but also the caring work was a constant drain on my strength. If at times when we met I seemed to be short-tempered and tired, if I seemed to lack understanding of your problems and not to give you the sympathy and encouragement you were needing, then I am truly sorry. It wasn't that I didn't *care*; it was simply that I lacked the energy, lacked the inner strength to cope with your suffering on top of my own. As I said, you need and deserve a woman who is stronger than I am – perhaps one who is more talented as well – and I hope and pray that you will find such a woman in the not too distant future.

As for me, I need now to put a closure to our experiences together. Our joys and sorrows, our hopes and fears, our worries and uncertainties. Closure does not mean forgetting any more than it means putting an end to love and friendship. Love *can* be false, it can be an illusion, but if it is true as ours is, it will live on. Live on way beyond our present lives on Earth, and – take my word for it – when these present lives are over we shall meet again on the other side. For me, if the doctors are right about this cursed consumption, that crossing over may come 'prematurely'. I must face that possibility, but at the same time I must bravely welcome and open myself up to the chance of new possibilities.

Please don't think that I have been 'brainwashed' against you. If I had really believed that being together was our destiny, that I was able to cope with all the difficulties that living with you would have brought, I would have stood up to my family and all the others. I would even have agreed to get married in a Roman Catholic Church! But no, when I look deep inside myself, I know that my family are right in thinking that New Zealand will be a better place for me to live. There is no way of knowing what the future may hold, but my aunt has written me the most welcoming of letters. She married well and has none of the financial constraints that beset, for instance, your family, and her family all sound to be ready to befriend me and to do all in their power to help me set myself up in a new and completely different sort of life. It is hard leaving you, my beloved, hard leaving my family and all that Worcester holds dear for me, but at the same time another side of me is excited. I have to admit it: bound up with my grief and with my anxiety about my health, is a determination to meet new challenges with fortitude. Just think of what those early settlers must have survived, sailing off 'into the blue' without the faintest idea of what lay in store! I at least shall have a welcoming party awaiting me when this ship finally docks in Auckland, a comfortable bed for the night... And at least there they speak English. It's not like Leipzig, where I struggled continually with the inadequacy of my German.

Now I am going to fold this letter, put it into an envelope and store it away with the forget-me-nots that you picked on that last walk we made together. I didn't tell you that I planned to press them and keep them safely in the trunk that I had already started packing. You were so distraught when you pleaded with me not to go that I could not bear to prolong the conversation, but just tucked the flowers away in my bosom, as you probably remember. Perhaps one day I shall open the envelope, re-read this letter and then burn it all, hoping that the smoke and the sentiments conveyed will somehow reach you on the ether.

In the meantime, one final x,

Nellie

No reply.

Little bit of old Leipzig.

It was difficult, in modern, busy, Leipzig, to get a sense of what
Edward and Helen saw there, but these may be some glimpses of it.

Site of the old Leipzig Conservatoire

**Site of Clara Schumann's birthplace. Both of these are
now shopping centres**

2 June 1889

Dear Ted,

First of all, Happy Birthday! Time has gone fast and I have been
busy. That does not mean that I have never given you another
thought. On the contrary: I heard recently from my brother
Frank that you were married. HUGE CONGRATULATIONS!
Frank did not give me any details, but I trust and pray that you
are happy and that your wife is giving you all the support you
need.

Just the other day I took out the letter that I wrote to you on
the ship and re-read it. I found it to express the sentiments I had
– indeed the sentiments I *still* have – fairly adequately. I am not
a born writer like you, any more than I am a born musician as
you are. I have to work hard at everything, as all the crossings
out and corrections in my previous letter show, but I did the best
possible job that I could in conveying my feelings and the difficulties I had been experiencing. That is why, especially now that

you are no longer single, I feel that it would still be wrong to put my letters into the post. By the way, the forget-me-nots are still safe in the envelope and, though not quite as blue as when you picked them for me, they are still a strong reminder of you!

I said I had been busy, and you may wonder how and why – especially if I admit that my violin has not come out of its case every day by any means. I told you that I was expecting a warm welcome in Auckland, and so it was. Despite my occasional pangs of nostalgia for our beautiful Worcestershire, I have found that New Zealand suits me. So much so in fact that I feel my health to have improved dramatically. For that I thank God. And I thank the New Zealand branch of my family for looking after me so well. They have taken me to visit *so* many interesting places. It truly is a fascinating as well as a beautiful country. If only you could see the Coromandel Peninsula, watch dolphins in the Bay of Islands, smell the sulphur and see the bubbling pools at the Craters of the Moon, or marvel as I have at the majesty of the mountains in the South Island. As for the kiwis (who only come out at night and aren't in the least bothered by human beings gawping at them), the podocarp forests and the glaciers and, returning now to the North Island, the *massive* kauri trees... And did you know that the robins here were entirely black?!

Then, besides all that, it's been an endless round of parties and socialising. To start with my aunt regularly invited groups of friends to her house to meet me, some of whom arranged for their children to come to me for violin lessons. This was good not only because it forced me not to abandon my practice all together, but also because it enabled me to earn a bit of pocket money and thus not be totally dependent upon my aunt's family's generosity. Then gradually, as I began to get stronger, I got included in a circle that entertains in all the poshest houses in the city. And I have to tell you that the quality of the food here is in general far superior to what most of us eat in England!

Now, dear Ted, I have a VERY big piece of news, which I hope and pray you will be happy to hear. I too am to be married; next year, I hope. The name of my betrothed is John Munro, he is a banker and, I assure you, he is a very *good* man. I don't love him in the way that I loved you – how could one? – but I do feel a genuine affection for him and I am quite confident that he will give me both the love and the security that I need. We both think too that it would be nice if we could have a family. He is twenty-nine just like me and, once he has turned thirty, his employers will permit him to marry.

Now that I've told you about myself, please, please tell me how you are. I know you won't send me a wedding present (I'm sure you couldn't afford to anyway!). I know you won't even write, but I would so like to know what you are up to. Apart from Frank having given me that brief piece of news about your marriage, my family never mention you in their letters. And I don't like to ask since I know it would make them worry that I was still pining for you, but I cannot help myself frequently wondering. Sometimes I lie awake at night visualising you battling with those tedious lessons. I don't suppose you'll ever get to really enjoy teaching! I am quite happy doing it, but your potential is for something *so* much greater. Sometimes I wonder whether you're making any real progress with your compositions. Maybe I'll never know! Silence is painful, but sometimes it just has to be endured. Anyway, I mustn't let these questions and concerns interfere with the new lives upon which we are both now embarking. I *do* hope you understand! Now I must stop because John is due to pick me up shortly as we're invited out to dinner at the Harrisons'.

Love as ever,

Nellie

P.S. No, I haven't yet acquired a New Zealand accent! Once, talking with a friend about the beauty of Ulva Island, I was baffled when she said, "Yes, it's our gym." Why would they want to make a gymnasium of an island?" I asked myself. Then, after a bit, it suddenly dawned on me that she actually meant "gem"!

Craters of the Moon, NZ North Island

Podocarp Forest, NZ South Island

27 December 1890

Afar, amidst the sunny Isles,
We dwelt awhile, my love and I.
Alice Elgar

Dearest Nellie,

First of all, Happy Birthday! Frank gave me the news of your marriage and I'm sorry it has taken me so long to send you my congratulations. But you will no doubt understand the mixed emotions that the news aroused in me and I therefore have no need to elaborate upon them. Instead, permit me to convey to you my own good news: I also was married (in Brompton Oratory in May last year) and my new status brings me much joy! Alice's aspirations for me as a composer, rather than an impecunious teacher and orchestral performer, caused us to move to London, which I shall never get to like as much as our beloved Worcestershire.

As I am sure you would have surmised, I had not been in a position to be able to afford to give up my teaching, and Alice came to me initially as a pupil. I cannot claim that it was 'love at first sight', for it took some months for the love between us to develop – especially since she is nine years my senior and so I could never have dreamt at first that she would take a serious interest in a 'youngster' such as myself – but now that our joint destiny has been sealed, I feel extremely content about it. Don't, however, think that our betrothal was straightforward. Alice's family are – just as you had hoped for me! – well-to-do, but they have from the start been strongly opposed to our liaison – for, need I say it, the precise same reasons as those expressed by your family. Her father, Major General Sir Henry Gee Roberts, who served in India where Alice was born, died when she was only twelve, but she has older brothers, a mother to care for, as well as aunts who are very influential. In fact so strong has been the latters' opposition to our match that one of them cut Alice off from the inheritance which was due to her. None of the family attended our wedding! So, in spite of Alice's small private income, 'church mice' we shall be, but determined not to let financial or family worries put us off or get in the way of my work. Do we not have a good role model in the Schumanns? Not that, please God, I anticipate ending my days in a mad house; just teaching in one has been quite enough for me! But I can also hold Robert as a musical role model, even if my dear Alice's pianistic abilities do not quite match those of Clara.

What else can I tell you about her? Well, without having Clara Schumann's genius, she has always nevertheless been a truly industrious student of the piano, and our love stemmed initially from the deep respect that we have for one another. She is something of a poet besides, and I have every intention of setting some of her poems to music. She has also had published a two-volume novel, entitled *Marchcroft Manor*. It received rather good reviews. Furthermore, she is remarkably good at watercolour painting. So you can see that all in all I am truly blessed with an exceptionally cultured wife! Can you guess what I gave her as an engagement present? You guessed right! It is only a trifle really – a delightful little tune that came to me when I was wandering that beautiful route which I feel sure you must still miss – but I am pleased with what I made of it, and she was absolutely thrilled to receive it. It is a setting of a poem that she wrote for me, and I entitled it *Liebesgrüss*.

I have now come to the belief that one can have more than one true love in one's life, but at the same time I am convinced that one loves them all differently. At one point I met a charming young lady up in Yorkshire and, though it came to nothing in the end – for the usual reasons! – I still hold fond memories of her. Just as I still do of you, and always shall. Yet my love for Alice, for Sarah-Anne and for you bear as little resemblance to each other as a Prelude and Fugue of the great Johann Sebastian, Beethoven's quartet Op. 130 and an opera of the revered Wagner. Such comparisons make no sense at all, do they?

But now I must tell you that the very best thing about dearest Alice is her complete and utter faith in me, not only as her music teacher, but – even more – for my compositions. For reasons best known to herself, she is absolutely convinced that I have the potential to be – can you believe it? – one of this country's "greatest ever" composers! And hand in hand with that conviction goes a determination to "see me make it". You will gather that she is a strong woman, and I have to face the fact that, as well as offering me constant love, companionship and consolation in my times of affliction (what you always called my 'black moods'!), she will keep me to the grindstone and never allow me to slacken. I can assure you that, if I ever do achieve anything of real note, it will be in very large part thanks to Alice.

Well, I had better stop there and return to elaborating some of those snippets that are scattered all around me!

Yours as ever,

Edward

7 October 1890

This is our meeting house for worship, here we are a
community connected by ties of faith and fellowship.
May the diversity of our beliefs be a blessing to share;
that all may grow in harmony with the Divine.
Celia Cartwright (From *Sing Your Faith*, Lindsey Press on behalf of The General Assembly of Unitarian and Free Christian Churches.)

Dear Edward,

Needless to say, Frank told me of your daughter's birth.

Congratulations to you both, and trust you to give her a unique name! Just Ann after your dear mother, or Lucy after one of your sisters, would never do for you – there are too many of them – but anyway Carice is pretty as well as unique and I'm sure your dear wife must be delighted all round. Do you pronounce the final 'e' on Irene – lovely too as a peaceful little girl's second name? I hope so!

As for me, I'm now proud and overjoyed to be a mother too. Do you know that almost as soon as we were wed, John and I moved to Patea? It was good in one way because John was appointed manager of the New South Wales bank here – quite a prestigious and secure post – but oh dear, I can't begin to tell you how much we've been missing our full life in Auckland. There's just hardly *anything* here! Fortunately people have been kind to us and I soon made a few friends, but I lack the stimulus, both musical and intellectual, that was available to me in Auckland. However, motherhood can only too easily be a full time job, and darling little Kenneth, just a month old today, is a great joy to me even though the lack of sleep sometimes gets the better of me. We are fortunate at least in having a housekeeper – a luxury that I imagine you and Alice cannot afford!

Anyway, while John was out at work all day and I was advised to rest a lot throughout my pregnancy, my thoughts inevitably turned to memories of you and our experiences together. How I missed you on Johann Sebastian's 200th birthday – if only we could have been in Leipzig together for the celebrations! But I shall never forget that day, quite some time before I set off for Leipzig, when I was minding the shop for father while he was feeling unwell and Mary Mercy, my stepmother, was busy attending to him. You came in because you were needing a new pair of shoes and so of course I had to serve you. You chose a smart pair of black ones, saying you needed them for appearing in concerts or teaching rather than for walking or golfing, and it suddenly hit me how very handsome you were. I suppose that up until then you had not been much more to me than Frank's talented friend. Playing only the violin and not a wind instrument, I couldn't join in with your "Sheds music making" behind your father's shop, but I was delighted when you named one of your compositions after me. I also found it amazing how you seemed to be able to turn your hand to just about any instrument, and it seemed such a pity that your family couldn't afford to send you off to one of the great music academies. But then, just as you were leaving with the shoebox under your arm and you asked me shyly to go for a boat ride with you the following Sunday, I felt glad that you were right there in Worcester rather than studying far away in, for instance, London or Leipzig! I didn't dare tell Papa about our date. I suppose that, even at that point, I somehow knew deep down that our relationship would get serious, and of course I knew too that – however, acceptable a Roman Catholic was as a friend for Frank – it would be quite another matter should it come to his being a suitor to his daughter. So, as you know, I told Papa and Mary Mercy a white lie about meeting "friends" after the church service.

Religious difference: what a strange and sad thing it is! I suppose you have *never* thought that it mattered very much, and of course in an ideal world it wouldn't. But alas we're a long way from living in an ideal world, and I'm afraid I simply can't stomach this 'Trinitarian' business. If there really is only one God, and all the major religions seem to be in agreement on that, then why on Earth should He/She divide Him/Herself into three? I'm sorry, but it just doesn't make any sense to me! I fully accept that Jesus was a wonderful example to humanity, a powerful healer and so on, but didn't he himself say that the one who sent him was greater than he was? Why do you Catholics have to elevate him to full Godhead and say that yours is the only way to salvation? I know that even your own father had no real respect for the Church. That's why you had to replace him as organist at

St George's after he failed to return soon enough from the pub following the sermon! I'm sure *he* wasn't as opposed to our marriage as my family were. Anyway, the religious factor wasn't the main obstacle for me: as I explained in the letter I wrote on the boat, it was more your unpredictable moodiness, combined with the total lack of financial security and my uncertain state of health that decided things for me. Alice was certainly braver than I am, though I cannot believe that she loves you any more than I did – and do! Of course I gather that she isn't a Catholic either, and that obviously wasn't an obstacle for you.

As for John and myself, well his Anglicanism isn't so strong that he's minded my not going along with it, and I had no objection to getting married in an Anglican church. I think we'll probably give our children a choice between allegiance to his Church or to mine. For yes, I would love to have a second child so long as my health permits it. We haven't actually got a Unitarian church here in Patea, but I shall certainly teach Kenneth about my own beliefs and let him make up his own mind when he is old enough. In any case, hopefully we won't be stuck here for ever. We'd both love to go back to Auckland one day. That's what I pray for, but right now my chief concern is care for Kenneth. No, I'm afraid the violin *hasn't* come out of her case since we moved. Marriage, moving house, pregnancy and child-birth are *quite* enough for a woman to cope with at one time!

But going back just for a moment to that first river outing of ours: do you remember what a lovely sunny day it was and that I was wearing my newest frock? It was blue of course! We were both rather shy – who wouldn't be on a first date? – but it was certainly on that day that I was suddenly precipitated into womanhood. Up until that point I had been too taken up with domestic preoccupations and chores, and trying to fit my violin studies in between them all, to give much thought to my burgeoning femininity. It was *you* who changed me overnight from a young girl into a woman! I had always thought that your hazel eyes were among the most exquisite and expressive that I had ever seen, but when they gazed into mine that day my heart melted completely and I knew that I could never, ever forget you, whatever happened later. You were so very handsome in your Sunday best and, although you didn't yet pluck up the courage to kiss me, you held my hand very tight as you helped me out of the boat and neither of us was in a hurry to drop our hands to our sides again. Are your hands still as beautiful now, by the way, as they were then? Probably! I was in ecstasy – that's no exaggeration – and I'm sure everyone noticed something when I got home again. Ah well, that's all the past now and there's no point in wasting time wondering what might have happened if I hadn't come to New Zealand. But occasionally I wonder whether you still enjoy flying kites. We had *so* much fun doing that together now and again, and something tells me that you will never completely abandon all your boyish traits!

Now Kenneth is crying and is no doubt due for a feed and nappy change. How I wish you could see what an adorable little mite he is!

Your ever loving Helen

As a respectable middle class wife and mother, I have to be Helen now! Anyway John doesn't really like 'Nellie'.

Park in Auckland

Coastline near Auckland.

26 June 1894

Dearest Helen,

Well, nothing came of our move to London and Alice's hopes of my starting on a 'proper' career there. Nobody seemed much interested in my work, I hated the hustle and bustle after the tranquil life and surroundings I was used to, and anyway I had plenty of teaching in both Malvern and Hereford. The travel to and fro was a strain and so it seemed to make much more sense to return to this part of the world. Having secured a house to rent in suburban Malvern, we settled quickly and my composing began to flow much more readily and constantly. Two works that I composed here have been well received – *The Black Knight* and *King Olaf* – and oh, how I wish that you could hear *From the Bavarian Highlands*. Knowing that country a bit yourself, I feel so sure that you would appreciate this work.

Alexandra Road, where our present house, Forli, is situated, is an extremely pleasant and quiet one, with a good number of fine houses in it. Forli is set back a bit from the road and, since dear little Carice is now well trained not to disturb me, I really have no excuse for not getting on with things. I hardly dare to say it, but I think I actually have quite a major and important work brewing. Of course I don't stay indoors all the time – especially at this time of year, when the countryside is so alluring – and anyway it is much easier to find inspiration outdoors than in. Sometimes I escape to what used to be some of *our* favourite haunts. Do you remember, for instance, that little secret spot I showed you by the River Teme at Knightwick? Right next to the Talbot Inn? Of course our massive Severn can be inspirational in its tranquil magnificence, but there is something so very intimate about its little sister Teme, and in my secret spot, dappled with light shining through its overhanging trees, its waters seem to babble with music.

Last night I dreamt about you in that very spot, which is what has prompted me to put pen to paper this morning even though I won't be able to post this when I've finished it. I was gazing into the water trying hard to catch its tune sufficiently to be able to write it down, when I suddenly looked up and saw that you were sitting right beside me. You were wearing that forget-me-not blue frock that I loved so much, and you were laughing at what I was saying about Schubert and his trout. You said that, even though you did very much enjoy the taste of trout, it would be really be better to let it stay in the river and just enjoy the music that it had inspired. Then in a flash you were gone. I turned round and saw that you were sitting on that old millstone, still looking very pretty as always, but with a pallor in your cheeks that I'd never noticed before. I got up to join you but, before I could do so, you had simply melted away.

River Teme at Knightwick, Worcs.

Old mill stone at Knightwick.

Upon awaking I lay still for quite some time reflecting on the dream and thinking about our relationship. It will soon be coming up to ten long years since you were gone, yet I can still see you as clearly as ever in my mind's eye and sometimes too I am strongly aware of your presence both in my sleeping and my waking hours. Sometimes I wonder whether you never really loved me as much as you said you did, but recently I've been chiding myself for perhaps not having shown enough under-standing of the difficulties that you had to go through. I feel sure now that you played down your illness, maybe because you were trying hard not to alarm either of us. Was it partly a fear of dying on me that prompted you to break off our engagement? I know that you always found my 'black moods' hard to cope with (well, I do too!), but was there was also a bit more to it than that? Please tell me that it was! Please tell me that you always loved me *and* that you never for a moment doubted my composing abilities! I just told you that I felt a truly great work brewing. Even if can never see you again, it needn't stop me from hoping that you will one day rejoice in my success.

Your ever loving,
Edward

4 July 1904

Art and music are thine own,
And thine the soul to whom must speak
The higher voices heard alone
By those who long and those who seek.
Alice Roberts (Elgar)

My dear Helen,

Dvorák is dead and we have moved house. The two are not connected. Or, on second thoughts, maybe they are in a strange sort of way?! Dvořák, as you may well appreciate, has always had such a big influence on me, I know full well that he and his music will be immortalised and, needless to say, I aspire to achieve that same immortality with my own works. I told you a few years ago, after one of many nostalgic dreams I had had about you, that I believed I had a great work brewing. Well, it happened! The *Enigma Variations* seem finally to have made my name, and now Alice has much cause to rejoice in her success. For, as I have always said, she is my ever-dependable rock without whom I might never have been able to aspire to anything worth remembering.

Tomorrow is American Independence Day, and it was in that country that the great Dvořák wrote some of his best works. I have no desire to leave my beloved Worcestershire to go and live in New York, which in any case I'm sure would be no better than London for my health, but if I am to approach Dvořák's success, I feel that our new abode, Plas Gwyn on the east side of Hereford, will be an ideal situation for realising it. Certainly Alice always hopes that a new abode will bring me new inspiration, and she says that she thinks great music can be written here. How I wish you could see my beautiful study here! Do you think I might be encouraged to compose a truly great symphony in this very room? How marvellous it would be if Beethoven and/or Brahms were to be proud of me. Then of course I have to write *your* violin concerto, not to mention another oratorio and a sort of sequel to my popular *Serenade for Strings*.

We were happy enough in our last home, 'Craeg Lea' in Malvern Wells, and I loved the view from it across the Severn Valley and over virtually the whole of Worcestershire, but living in Hereford has various advantages – not least the fact of it being of course triennially one of the venues for my beloved Three Choirs Festival. Malvern *is* good for music, but it has no cathedral, and I especially love Hereford's Romanesque nave. Whether or not my good architect friend Troyte, featured of course in my Variations, would agree with me, I think even those great Gothic architects were hard put to beat their Norman predecessors. By the way, 'Craeg Lea' is an anagram, composed by me of course, of our three names. Dear Carice is fourteen now and is still boarding at The Mount, Rosa Burley's school in Malvern. Rosa, by the way, is a good friend of ours, a good walking companion for me, and I trust Carice totally to her care.

View from Craeg Lea, Malvern Wells, Worcs.

Minafon, owned by Elgar's friend Alfred Rodewald

Rivers were always very important for Elgar, and the Conwy runs past the bottom of the Garden of Minafon

Yes, tomorrow is American Independence Day and you will never guess what is happening the day after: I am to be knighted! I have to go to Buckingham Palace to meet the King of course. I expect it'll be a bit of a bore really, but what pleases Alice – what she's worked so d----d hard for – must perforce please me. One really sad thing about it is that my dear mother is no longer alive to see this. Death is such a terribly difficult thing to have to cope with, and I don't think the Church really gives us much help with it in their prayers for "eternal rest"! Why should we want eternal rest? Don't you think it sounds boring? It was bad enough when my beloved dog Scap died, and Alice has never wanted me to get another dog even though Carice would love us to have one, but losing one's mother is even worse. Still, that's something I don't need to tell *you*! At least, unlike you, I was lucky enough to have her around until after I had reached my forties, and I can always be grateful for her influence on me. Like Alice, she had literary talents, which I suppose I have inherited as well as my father's musical ones, and I certainly also inherited her great love of the countryside. In fact I would dearly love to have the time to make more use of my literary talents, as well as of my other interests such as chemistry, but something has always driven me into music. I suppose it must be destiny – if there is such a thing. Didn't the Greeks describe it as the *daimon*?

Then, before I had had time to recover from the loss of my dear mother, I suffered another really terrible one only the following year. I've never told you about my great friend Alfred Rodewald from Liverpool. He was a cotton merchant, but also an exceptionally gifted amateur musician – so good in fact that he should really have been a professional. He studied conducting under Richter and formed his own orchestra in his adopted city. As his name implies, he was of German blood, but he was born in this country. Granville Bantock was responsible for our meeting because he invited me to give a concert of my own works in Liverpool, and 'Rodey', as most of us call him, was in the audience. We made friends instantly because Rodey understood my music so perfectly. He also owned a house in a most beautiful spot in North Wales, on the river Dee and close to Betws-y-Coed, and we were invited for some truly memorable holidays there. When I was working on my oratorio *The Apostles* I trusted Rodey so totally that I gave him some of my drafts to comment on, which he did very usefully, and I dedicated my first 'Pomp and Circumstance March' to him. By the way, I have a strong feeling that those successful and popular Marches wouldn't be your favourites of my works, but even you would have to admit that *Land of Hope and Glory* is a truly splendid tune! It appears to give the British people something that they feel they need now that the Empire seems to be beginning to crumble, and it's certainly a darned sight better than the National Anthem.

Anyway, Rodey and I had only been able to know each other and get close for four years when he suddenly fell ill and died totally unexpectedly. He was only forty-one and so I had counted on having him as an advisor and support for the rest of my life. We had visited each other a number of times, as well as having those wonderful Welsh holidays that I'll never forget, and so I rushed straight up to Liverpool the moment I heard he was ill, in November last year, but I got there too late. I'm sure you can imagine how distressed I was – and still am – and I don't know that I'll ever feel inclined to visit that part of Wales again, much though I fell for it. Rodey had a car that he was rather proud of, but it kept breaking down, so it got nicknamed 'the Shover' and it failed to convert me away from foot or bicycle. Poor Alice once had a nightmarish evening at Minafon, when we had failed to return and had to spend the night in Corwen! I was asked to write an obituary for Rodey, but declined because writing about him would have accentuated my pain. Anyway music is my best medium and so the slow movement of my second symphony is

Mary Hofman and Richard Ormerod playing the Elgar Violin Sonata to members of the West Midlands Branch of the Elgar society on their summer jaunt, 2013. For me it would be easier to believe that Mary was previously Helen than that I was!

his memorial.

If there really is a God, why does He take our nearest and dearest away from us without apparent reason? Your faith always seemed so strong; I wish you could help me! Well, on that sad note I will close, trusting that your two offspring are now growing up nicely and bringing you great joy.

Your ever loving,

Edward

Their appreciative audience in the sitting room at Minafon

28 December 1905

Dearest Edward,

Yesterday was my forty-fifth birthday and you'll never guess how I celebrated it! Dear John had a bit of work to do at the bank in Auckland and so he brought Joyce and me with him and bought a couple of concert tickets. Kenneth has just gone off to board at Nelson College and John's parents were quite happy to look after Joyce for the evening. No, we didn't waste a lot of time in having a second child and are extremely happy with our 'pigeon pair'. Joyce will be twelve very soon and is a truly delightful child. I miss Kenneth of course, but he's a bright lad and we're naturally keen for him to get the best education available.

Anyway, it was a wonderful concert and guess what they played: the *Enigma Variations*! So Edward, you've finally made it! This is more than I'd ever dared to hope for you, though certainly *not* more than you deserve. What an amazingly unique and wonderful work it is! The programme notes they provided were quite detailed and I've been reading them and re-reading them. Now I just can't wait to hear the work played again. I've just acquired a rather good gramophone, so I hope I'll soon be able to buy some records of it. How *incredibly* clever of you to make that Dan variation sound so *exactly* like a dog in the river! Not our beloved Severn, I noticed, but the no doubt equally lovely Wye, which I know less well of course. As for the self-portrait at the end, well the power of it is quite staggering. It's saying so assertively, "This is who I am. I'm the great musician and composer Edward Elgar. You can love me or hate me, but now that I've found myself I'm not going to change."

But who is this Lady Mary Lygon of Variation number XIII? They say in these notes that I'm re-reading yet again that the asterisks denote a woman who is off on a sea journey – hence your quotation from Mendelssohn's 'Calm Sea and a Prosperous Voyage' – but if that's the case, why on Earth didn't you write out her name? It's not something you're ashamed about, is it? You haven't been having a clandestine affair? No, surely not! I *know* you and I'm quite sure that you would never be unfaithful to your dear Alice. So could it possibly be…? Dare I ask this? Could those asterisks really denote the name Helen? That would make much more sense because, if LML is known as a good friend of yours, you'd have absolutely no reason to hide it. Whereas if you were actually thinking of me… If you still felt a tiny bit the same about me as before (as, I have to admit, I do of you even after all this time), then of course you'd have every reason to hide the said lady's identity! As I listened to that particular variation, having had time to read through the programme notes before the concert started, my heart missed a beat – maybe even several beats – and I swear that when I heard that extraordinary drum roll I thought it sounded exactly like the engine of the ship that brought me away from England.

What more have I to say? Nothing right now except that I trust and hope that you will go on to write more works as great as this one. I do so love those part songs, especially *My Love Dwelt in a Northern Land*, and of course *Salut d'Amour* is pure delight, but the *Enigma* are SOMETHING ELSE – a sign of TRUE GREATNESS. By the way, is it true that *Salut d'Amour* was originally entitled *Leibesgrüss*? I could understand your giving it a German title following your visits to that land, but maybe French is considered more fashionable these days?

Well, John should be back shortly so I'll say farewell for the time being.

Your ever loving,

Helen

12 March 1906

Don't ask yourself what the world needs. Ask yourself what makes you come alive. What the world needs is truly alive people.
Howard Thurman

My dear Helen,

I heard the other day that my *Enigma Variations* had received rapturous applause and reviews after being performed in Auckland, so I couldn't help wondering to myself whether by any chance you were able to get to that concert. In fact I have to admit that my imagination has been running wild visualising you sitting there in the audience and really enjoying it. Sadly it probably is just wild imagination because the last news that Frank gave me was that you were living somewhere on the other side of the country. I do wish you could hear them, though, because these Variations are something that I'm really proud of. I had a lot of fun writing the work; it's quite a challenge making musical portraits of one's best friends, but I feel I rose to the challenge quite satisfactorily. If only you *were* able to hear the work performed, I wonder whether you'd be able to guess that you were enshrined in it as well. I like to think that you would realise because I shall never divulge your identity, but rather let people just go on surmising about it. The consensus seems to be that my asterisks represent my good friend Mary Lygon, though why they should think that I might feel a need to conceal *her* identity is a mystery to me. Anyway, let them think what they will; what matters to me is that so many people are really excited about the work and recognise its (though I say it myself!) exceptionally good orchestration. The identity of Variation XIII, by the way, is not the only enigma: permeated through the whole of the work is an enigmatic theme – one that I think *you* just might be able to guess correctly; I'll say no more on that subject!

Now that I've got that off my chest, I really want to tell you that I've been busy for a while writing a violin concerto for you. I don't know when it will be finished. It may take some time yet because it's got to be really good. I'm not Mozart! Nor would I want to be for that matter; for one thing, if I were Mozart I'd already have been dead for thirteen years. No, with me the music never just pours out like milk from a jug. Do you remember my habit of jotting down little bits and pieces all over the place whenever they came into my head? Well, noting down pretty little tunes, beautiful melodies or sonorous chords and harmonies is one thing; subsequently putting them all together apparently seamlessly is quite another! I assure you: that takes a great deal of work, and if it weren't for my good wife tirelessly ruling out my manuscript paper and keeping me at it – often when I'd rather be out cycling the Malvern Hills* – I'd probably never get any work finished at all. It's an awful lot of work for poor Alice, but buying the paper ready lined is so expensive and we're still always strapped for cash, alas!

At least here in peaceful Plas Gwyn I have, as I believe I told you in a previous letter, the pleasantest of studies you could ever imagine for working in, and the views from our windows and balconies are inspirational. Maybe one day they'll put more buildings up around here, which will be a great shame. There's no escape from so-called 'progress' and more houses will always be needed by a growing population, but I just hope it won't be while we're here! So, if ever you do hear of a violin concerto by EE, please, please, make an effort to hear it, and please appreciate it is *your* soul that is therein enshrined. Its period of gestation, which again I mentioned in my letter of last year, was a long one, but I hope the world will feel it to have been well worth waiting for. We may not have been destined to share a life together, but that work will be our joint legacy to the world of violin lovers.

Yours as ever,
Edward

*Walking these hills too, as you would no doubt appreciate, is one of my greatest sources of inspiration. My *Introduction and Allegro for Strings*, of which I have to say I am immensely proud, is walking music, and of course that was put onto paper here in my lovely study at Plas Gwyn.

15 September 1909

Dear Edward,

Kenneth has been doing so well at school. We are immensely

proud of him. A couple of years ago he was made a prefect and now, in his final year, they have made him Head Prefect. There looks to be a good chance that, once he finishes at Nelson College, he will go on to study Law at Victoria College in Wellington. At least that will be bit closer for us. Joyce is developing into a lovely young girl too. We are blessed with our children, as I hope you and Alice are with Carice.

Now, following on from my rapture over your amazing Variations a very, very different work has come to my attention: *Caractus*. Is it true that the idea for it came from your good mother, as she was gazing at the Herefordshire Beacon and the British Camp atop it? I dare say she has passed on, and no doubt you miss her. I know it was written earlier – before you had grown fully into your complete mastery of both orchestra and chorus – but it still has that unmistakably Elgarian stamp. All the Pomp and Circumstance. (Not that those Marches are nearly as much to my taste as, say, your songs!) I was impressed when I heard it, parts of it moved me deeply, BUT there was one tiny snippet that I found, I can only say, tantalising. You must know the bit I mean! It's entitled *Woodland Interlude*. The best description I can think of for it, not having your mastery of the English language, is a little wisp of beautiful white smoke that I want to grasp and hold on to, but which has simply melted away before I've managed to get anywhere near it.

Edward, why did you do that? What were you trying to say? That true happiness in life is never anything more than a few seconds of bliss, which we have glimpsed momentarily and has then been whisked away from us? I wish we could meet – if only for five minutes – so that you could explain your intention to me. Because you have not to my knowledge done anything at all like that anywhere else. You are an absolute master of utterly beautiful melody, but normally you ground your melodies, you let us get hold of them – own them even, as you embroider them with your wonderful gold and silver threads – but in that tiny bit of

Caractacus there's nothing like that. Okay, after the chorus comes in following those will o' the wisp few bars from the orchestra, there is another little hint of the tune – if you can even call it a tune! – but then once more it disappears from view before we've had the chance to be fully aware of its presence. What is it? A glimpse of Heaven? An angel? What were you *feeling* when you wrote it? Maybe, Edward dear, I shall never know.

I know there's been quite a gap in my letters, but life gets full! Anyway John is due home from work now and I must present him with a meal that will be satisfying for his weary body and mind, not tantalising!

Love,
Helen

The Herefordshire Beacon

Mordiford Bridge, near Hereford, where Elgar loved to fish

4 August 1916

> *What passing-bells for these who die as cattle?*
> *Only the monstrous anger of the guns.*
> *Only the stuttering rifles' rapid rattle*
> *Can patter out their hasty orisons...*
> Wilfred Owen, *Anthem for Doomed Youth*

My dearest Helen,

How can I express my sympathy over Kenneth's death? You and John must be really shattered by it, and I too am feeling extremely distressed. When he was invalided to Hampstead and came to visit, I welcomed him almost as though he were my own son. There was so much of you in him, and I thought we made good friends in what was really a very short space of time. What a cruel war this is – taking so much precious life so prematurely!

It must have been bad enough for you when Kenneth set off for such distant lands, and now to have lost him all together... It's unthinkable! Will you all be coming over to Europe to visit the grave once the war is over and travel becomes less difficult again?

Oh the futility of it all. I just can't bear to think about how many lives have been lost. You cannot imagine how despondent it has made me. On second thoughts maybe *you* can imagine! And, on top of my depression triggered by this terrible war, my tonsillitis has been so troublesome again and I have recurring eye problems. But who am I to complain about troubles? At least my daughter is alive and well and won't be despatched to the Forces! Last year I started composing a work that I am calling *The Spirit of England*; it is dedicated "To the memory of our glorious men, with special thought for the Worcesters'", and of course I include Kenneth in the Worcesters' since his maternal lineage made him "one of us". I think you would like the work and be proud of me. Even if it is less to your taste than, say, *Is she not passing fair? Where Corals Lie* from the *Sea Pictures*, or *The Dream of Gerontius*. I know that the latter is my absolute masterpiece to date, even though its first performance in Birmingham was disastrous and threw me into such a dreadful depression. I feel you would love the *Music Makers* too, if only you could hear it. I composed some of it while I was fishing at Mordiford bridge near Hereford – a lovely spot that I discovered only after you had left England; how I wish that I could introduce you to it! Some people are critical of O'Shaughnessy's poem, but parts of it really *speak* to me. "We are the music makers, and we are the dreamers of dreams..." Was that not *us*, you and me together, all those years ago? Playing our violins and dreaming of a wonderful future together...

You remember our concert-going when I had that wonderful holiday in Leipzig just after your 21st birthday? Well, I suppose you've heard about the Gewandhaus being rebuilt – not so long after you had left Leipzig? It needed to be! No doubt it is now a much more comfortable venue for enjoying concerts, and perhaps if we had gone later we would have had the additional pleasure of being able to sit together, but the standard of the music making when we were there was of course very high. A bit of me would like to return and experience the new Gewandhaus, but I fear that your absence would make me feel too sad. Although I knew you deserved it of course, I envied you being able to study at the Conservatoire, only a stone's throw from Clara Schumann's birthplace. If only my father's business had been as profitable as yours, my parents might have been able to afford for me to go there too. As it is I've just had to slog away at teaching myself composition. Ah well!

Leipzig – *what* a place! You must remember too the reverence we both felt sitting in the St Thomaskirche, listening to Johann Sebastian's very own choir. Isn't it wonderful that the Leipzig Boys' Choir is still going strong after having been founded so long ago – in 1284?! During that blissful two weeks you seemed so sure that our destiny would be together. How I wonder what would have happened if you hadn't changed your mind. *Could* we have gone on being as happy as were in Leipzig, or would my dreadful moodiness have spoilt the romance? And what of my composing career? Would I have 'made it' if I had been happy all the time? Could Brahms have written his Requiem if his mother hadn't died and if he'd been happily married to Clara? How much of the best poetry has sprung from profound grief?

I suppose really that it was lack of emotional fulfilment that could be held responsible for the loveliest of my songs. *So* many people have said how beautiful they have found them that there is no point in being modest. No, if I'm perfectly honest, modesty is not my strongest point! Talking of song, someone asked me the other day whether I was much influenced by folk music. I thought it was rather a silly question and so I replied, "I AM folk music." I think they were a bit taken aback, but why should I care what people think? Especially those music critics – they haven't got a clue, most of them!

Emotional fulfilment: I hear you asking, "What about Alice?" Well, as I've told you before, Alice is a good woman and I depend on her for everything that's most important in my life, but ... I wonder whether you'd agree with me – I feel you would – that somehow one's first love overshadows everything. Even when I first fell in love with dear Alice – and I *do* still love her – I knew that there would never be the same romantic element in the relationship as in that I'd had with you. Maybe I'm *too much* of a romantic! But could I be a true Romantic (worthy of the aforesaid Johannes B!) if I weren't also so romantic?

So no, it's difficult for my good, practical, dedicated Alice fully to understand that side of me. Consequently, though I'd never dream for a moment of being unfaithful to her, I could no doubt be accused of having something of a wandering eye. We artists need lady friends to inspire and nurture the feminine aspect of our work and, being unable to go as far as New Zealand, my eye lighted a few years ago upon another Alice, whose character could hardly be more different than that of Alice Elgar. She is the daughter of the painter Millais and married to a gentleman by name of Stuart Wortley, the MP for Sheffield. That gives a double reason for our relationship being purely Platonic, but we have a mutual understanding that has, I think, helped my music to flourish recently. I have nicknamed her Windflower, which feels most appropriate, and of course it distinguishes her in my mind from my good wife. Another excellent female friend I have is Dora Penny, whom I named Dorabella in the Variations, after Mozart's Dorabella of course. But she is merely a girl – someone with whom I can a lot of fun, *when* I'm in the mood for fun.

Which is not right now, while I'm feeling so oppressed by this ghastly war, devastated by the news of your Kenneth's death, angry and depressed about the cruelty to horses that's been going on as well as by the futile loss of young human life, and in fact worried as to whether I'll even manage to finish *The Spirit of England*, let alone ever compose anything else of note. Do you know that I signed up as a Special Constable in Hampstead in a frenzied bid to actually do something useful? But I'm afraid I soon had to give it up as I found the night duty simply too taxing. Maybe putting everything that's going on into music is an equally good way to be of service? I don't know, but I know that it's what I have to do and pray to God (if there *is* a God!) that what I succeed in putting on to paper will endure. I suppose my chief aim at the moment is to hand on to future generations at least some little inkling of what we are going through.

Kenneth no doubt told you something about Severn House; we changed the name from Kelston to make me feel more at home. We bought it in 1912, when a return to London seemed to make sense because of the work I get here. Moving house is tiresome, to put it mildly, but sometimes leases run out, which was of course a good reason for buying this time. It is a truly splendid house, which accords totally with Alice's upper class upbringing – that's mainly why she chose it of course – but I do find the endless entertaining very wearing. She, however, regards entertaining bigwigs as very important. I suppose she's right really in a way, now that my work is finally recognised in this country for what it's worth. Alice is no cook, but she is extremely good at organising help from others and at making the house look impressive. Well, she was never taught to cook as my sisters were; class system *again* – the bane of our society!

Alice, like you, appreciates the extent to which I am affected by my surroundings, and – though I am sometimes sorely tempted to pack this music lark in all together and have more time to indulge some of my other interests – exercise still often gives me inspiration. Walking on Hampstead Heath is some sort of substitute for my beloved Malverns, but I can't help being a little envious of people who come here with their dogs. In addition, however, since Alice appreciates the extent to which Severn House is more to her taste than mine, she has acquired the rental of a lovely little cottage in Sussex, named Brinkwells. It reminds me of my beloved Birchwood and I can compose there in peace.

Expressing true feelings – that is to say one's *real* self rather than things one thinks that the public wants, such as 'Pomp and Circumstance' – is far from easy. Perhaps it's particularly difficult for an Englishman since we're supposed to have this 'stiff upper lip' all the time; those poor young men are expected to march off proudly to defend their country and they simply aren't allowed to divulge their fears and apprehensions to *anyone*. They even get severely punished for cowardice if they show signs of having been traumatised! So, as I say, expressing one's real, suffering self is far from easy, but I did it right at the beginning of this war, in a tiny little work I named *Sospiri*. I wrote that following the death of Julia Worthington; we knew her as 'Pippa' and she was someone else I always felt close to. Somehow an Italian name seemed more fitting than 'Sighs'; maybe it's because Italians are better than we are at showing their feelings. I'd expressed the real me before of course – especially in parts of *Gerontius* – and in *Caractacus*, my first major choral work, I steered very briefly completely from the main tone by inserting a minute *Woodland Interlude*, which is really, I suppose, a little glimpse of the happiness I shared with you. It was inspired by the trees around where we were living at the time*; they seemed to be singing my music, though I was never quite sure whether it was that or whether I had sung theirs. My dear mother had suggested my using that subject when she was holidaying in a cottage in Colwall, where she could look out on to the Herefordshire Beacon and the British Camp, which, as you may remember, is where *Caractacus* made his last stand. Brief though it is, I have to say that I really love my *Woodland Interlude*; I think I may want to have it played to me when I'm on my deathbed!

I wonder how you feel about our great British Empire now that you are ensconced in more or less the furthest corner of it? Anyway, whether or not you are proud of that, I'm sure that you would have been proud of *me* when I was commissioned to write my masque *The Crown of India*! It was intended to commemorate the royal visit to Delhi in November 1911, when George V and Queen Mary were crowned Emperor and Empress of India. The libretto is by Henry Hamilton and it had its first performance at the London Coliseum in March 1912. I have to say that two weeks of twice daily rehearsals wore me out, and Alice was quite worried about it all. But then Alice frequently worries about my health – not without good cause – and this particular occasion was worth all the time and effort put into it.

Then 1913 saw the first performance of *Falstaff*, a great orchestral work in which my soft spot for the military can be detected. This work displays at the same time the dreamy side of my (admittedly complex!) character. I was keen here to put the other side to Shakespeare's somewhat unfair depiction of poor old Falstaff. His is of course a very sad story, but I firmly believe that he could be brave even if he was a coward sometimes. However, when I refer to it as a "great orchestral work", that does not, alas, mean that the whole of the musical world agrees with me! In fact some people who I really think ought to know better just don't seem to understand it at all.

And on that sad note, wishing so desperately that I could *do* something for you in your inevitable grief, I must end this missive. A missive that of course I could not post even if I had an address for you, but putting one's feelings into a letter can be cathartic in the same that way that composing music can be.

Your ever loving,

Edward

---

*I wrote much of *Caractacus* for the prestigious Leeds Triennial Festival and, like *Sea Pictures* and *The Dream*, I wrote it at Birchwood Lodge, the lovely house out in the wilds near Malvern, that we lived in for about three years from 1898, which has a splendid view looking north-west towards Bredon Hill. It was there, too, that I learnt to ride a bicycle, and that of course considerably extended the range of places I could go in search of inspiration.

No reply. (What could Helen say when she was so grief stricken by her son's death?)

The St. Thomas Kirche, where J.S. Bach worked for so long

J.S. Bach's tomb, which I'm sure EE and HW will have
venerated together

Birchwood Lodge

View from Birchwood Lodge

15 September 1919

My dear Helen,

After your son's death I endeavoured to express to you my
sympathy over the loss, but I know that I was unable to do that
at all adequately on account of all the suffering that I myself was
going through at the time. I think I told you that, on top of all the
misery of that wretched war, I was suffering both with recurrent
eye problems and from tonsillitis. Well eventually, last year,
those confounded tonsils flared up so badly that the doctors
decided there was nothing to be done except remove them. I
can't tell you how painful it was. My throat was literally on fire
with soreness and I thought I would die of starvation because
eating anything of substance was impossible. However, I am
delighted to say that I am now recovered and pretty much back
to my good-humoured self. And one really good thing came out
of the operation besides the most troublesome bit of my body
having been brutally extracted! Just as I was slowly coming
round from the anaesthetic, a tune *quite* unlike any other began
to form itself in my head. Do you think it might be possible that
on occasions such as a painful operation one's soul detaches itself
from the body and makes a brief escape? If so, I think I may have
gone up to Heaven and been given the gift of this rather extraordinary tune! Anyway, I hung on to it for dear life until I was
safely home again and able to bash it out on my beloved
Broadwood. Then I wrote it down for Windflower, and gradually
the theme moved from the piano to the 'cello. After that, to my
great satisfaction, I elaborated upon it and kept adding more and
more bits until eventually I found to my amazement that I had
composed a full 'cello concerto. It is now being published and I
have a feeling that it might in due course even exceed *your*
concerto in popularity, though not, I think, deservedly! Well,
much though we both love the violin, the 'cello has the most

wonderful richness that cannot be matched by any other instrument, don't you think?

So yes, if only I were able to contact you, and if only you had got over your intense grief, I hope you would be happy to hear that I have now emerged from a particularly lengthy 'black mood'. The ending of the war was of course an immense relief, even though the devastating consequences of it are still so evident, but also I think I can now tell you in all honesty that I really have finally 'made it' as a composer, just as you used to dream for me. I think you appreciate just how important the Three Choirs Festival is to me, and now I feel confident that performances of *Gerontius* will be pretty much a regular feature of it, even if my other oratorios fail to gain quite the recognition they deserve. Well, I suppose *The Apostles*, with its six soloists, will always seem expensive to put on!

And, to prove my point about having 'made it', I should like to recount to you a conversation I overheard at the most recent Three Choirs Festival. It was a discussion – nay, I could even say a heated argument – between two musicologists who shall be nameless as to who was the "greatest English composer", Henry Purcell or my good self! Of course a more absurd topic to argue about could hardly be imagined, but I felt, needless to say, immensely flattered to be mentioned in the same breath as the great Purcell! I did not wish to embarrass them by making my presence known (they were sitting behind me in the cathedral and I suppose failed to recognise the back of my head!), but had I felt a desire to intervene, I would have pointed out to them the absurdity of the comparison. I am sure you would agree!

For – whether or not I do truly deserve to be ranked with Henry Purcell – how can one compare chalk with cheese? Chalk and cheese each have their uses, but these are as different as the ingredients from which they are constituted. Purcell, as we well know, was a seventeenth century composer and his beautiful works could not have emerged from any other era, but who would want *me* to compose in the style that he did? Things have changed radically since those times and I have to be a voice of *our* time! Besides, they were discussing the merits of "Purcell and Elgar", yet what of the recently deceased Hubert Parry, or Gustav Holst with his Indian, Hindu interests, now back from his musical war efforts in the Near East and engaged by more than one esteemed university? Or again, some would no doubt say, what of William Byrd or Orlando Gibbons? Or, moving forward yet more, even my good friend Ralph Vaughan Williams seems to be showing a great deal of promise! Some people of course claim the great Handel as English, but that is cheating in my opinion. Our having adopted him doesn't mean that his Teutonic roots were obliterated. When Alice and I had our wonderful holidays in Bavaria I found it easy to understand why that country had produced a larger number of the greatest composers than any other!

How could anyone say who is the greater of Mozart or Beethoven, Strauss or Wagner? I turn to Tchaikovsky when I'm feeling gloomy, to Mozart when I want to be lifted out of despondency, to Bach when I am searching for God (never easy at the best of times!), to Beethoven when I want to be stimulated intellectually – well, to Johann Sebastian also for that of course – to Wagner when I'm in one of my grandiose moods, to Mahler when I'm feeling expansive... I would never compare any of them with each other. Each serves a different purpose, just as Purcell and I do.

I think a big distinction can be made between the Arts and Science because, whereas in the latter one can talk of 'advancement' or 'progress', with the former all those who practise them are products of their particular age. If new scientific discoveries were not made – if people did not make improvements – we would still all have to rely on horses for our transport and we would not have electricity. But how could anyone ever *improve* on a Greek temple, a Leonardo painting, a

Shakespeare play or sonnet, the slow movement of the Bach double concerto or Dido's *Lament*? Each is a child of its time that could not have been birthed at any other time. Where the genius lies – and this can of course also apply to, say, Isaac Newton, is when the artist transcends time as well as speaking from and for it. This is what Henry Purcell was able to do with his music; this is what I aim to do with mine. I cannot hazard a guess as to whether my work will speak to future generations as it appears to be doing to ours, but to create things that will last is my dream, just as I imagine it was Purcell's. To choose between us for greatness is to me a nonsense; but if you were proud of me it would give me great joy.

Your ever loving,

Edward

I am still at heart the dreamy child who used to be found in the reeds by Severn side with a sheet of paper trying to fix the sounds & longing for something very great.

EE writing to Sidney Colvin, 13 December 1921

27 December 1920

Dearest Helen,

Your birthday today; you see how I never forget, even when I'm in the depths of despondency. And maybe Frank told you the reason for my present despondent state. My dear Alice – that's my wife, not Windflower – died earlier this year. I cannot begin to tell you about the emotions I have been through since her departure: riddled with grief, loneliness and guilt. The first two may seem to you – especially after your own tremendous losses – completely natural. The last is caused by a multitude of things: the fact that *I* should have been able to detect her cancer earlier, my appalling feelings of inadequacy in caring for her adequately once it had been realised that she was seriously ill, the fact that, especially in recent years, I had been enjoying the company of other women more than hers, my lack of appreciation of all the work that she put into me... It's never ending and I don't think I shall ever be able to forgive myself. One can't really blame Alice for having got a bit boring when she had taken on so much.

So you see, dear Helen, forget fame, my knighthood (which mattered much more to Alice anyway than it ever did to me), my briefly-held Chair at Birmingham University, and the fact that I 'made it' in accordance with yours and Alice's hopes. I am now a broken man. All inspiration has left me and I cannot see that I shall ever compose again. This despite the fact that I still have fragments of what should be a good piano concerto lying all over the place, and that people are urging me to write a third symphony. I'm dedicating the slow movement of the embryonic piano concerto to my dear Alice Stuart Wortley, who has done much to fill the gap that you left. The Three Choirs will be coming up again in just a few months and no doubt a new work for it is expected from me. What can I do? The poet needs his muse and, when I look pleadingly at Alice's photo, nothing is forthcoming. She, by the way, called the slow movement of my string quartet "captured sunshine". Isn't that lovely? Oh how I'd love to play it with you!

And as well as all my present "mouldiness", as Alice used to call it, I'd like to tell you about something that makes me really angry and has done for years. It's the fact that people are for ever talking about my having a "chip on my shoulder". "Chip on my shoulder" – as though the discrimination to which I have been subjected all my life were *my* fault rather than that of English society! Is it right that *anyone* – whether or not they have a lot of talent – should be judged by the circumstances, family or religion into which they happen to have been born? It's different now – now that my work has been recognised for its qualities – but how can I ever forget the struggle I had to achieve it? No honorary degree, no knighthood, no Master of the King's Music (a thing to which I may yet aspire), no invitation to compose for a ceremonial occasion will ever erase all that for me. If I had been born into a well-to-do Anglican family, I could have gone to study in Leipzig as I so wanted, or at least to some other good music school, rather than having to teach myself *everything*, and acquiring a wife would have been easier for me. Yet, rather than acknowledging what I had to contend with, people just say to one another, "Edward Elgar has a huge chip on his shoulder"! All I can hope now is that future generations will become more open-minded and tolerant, so that young people can be offered opportunities according to their abilities rather than their background.

And on that disgruntled and self-pitying note I will close, but not without alluding to the fact that at times I still miss and mourn my loss even though it is John's and New Zealand's gain.

Yours as ever,

EE

Long silence.

2 June 1924

> *We walk no more, we talk no more*
> *Each dwells on far divided shore*
> *The hours are dull and life seems told*
> *A dream unreal of years of old.*
> *So far away*
> *Is yesterday.*
> Alice Roberts (from 'Yesterday')

Dear Edward,

Your birthday today, which prompts me to put pen to paper for the first time since my darling son lost his life in France, a sacrificial victim in the name of Freedom. Eight long years, during which my husband and I have lost both our children! What have I done to deserve such suffering? First I lost both my parents before my twenty-first birthday, then the stepmother to whom I was close, then (through my own fault, I admit) the love of my life, then my only son, whom I had not even seen since he left home for Europe, and finally my only daughter. Yes, as though losing Mary Mercy to consumption and then falling victim to it myself hadn't been enough, that same disease then stole from us our beloved Joyce at the tender age of twenty-eight. I have been so grief stricken that all my zest for life has been drained away and even now it is only with the greatest difficulty that I can summon the effort to wish you a Happy Birthday. And what is the point of making even this small effort when I cannot bring myself then to post this letter conveying my good wishes to you?

I wonder what's happening today in Worcester and/or Malvern. Are they organising a birthday concert in your honour? Now there is no Alice of course to organise a celebration; at least you still have Carice, but is she able, now that she's married, to give you what you need on this special day? I hear so little from Frank now that he has abandoned his family and business, and there is really no one else I can ask for news of you. I wonder whether you are doing any composing to speak of. Did you ever think of writing a Requiem for Alice, or would that have been too painful? Ever since hearing the sad news of her demise, I've thought so often about the grief you must be suffering, even sometimes chiding myself for feeling so sorry for *my*self. After all, I at least still have John standing by my side.

After the war was over there was talk of the three of us going to visit Kenneth's grave in Armentières – John would have liked to anyway – but I just couldn't have faced the long journey. You see, my health is rather up and down again these days, and the other two didn't fancy going without me. In any case I didn't think there was a lot of point because it's not as though *he* was there. What is the body but a shell that we cast off when our time has come, and the fact that Kenneth's time came early doesn't make any real difference. His spirit has been around all the time; I have never doubted his presence and feel that he hears me when I talk to him in my mind. That – combined with the knowledge that he fought bravely for an important cause and that his death was not totally in vain – has brought me a certain amount of consolation during these eight long years.

I am so very glad that you and Kenneth at least got to know one another before he was killed! He wrote to me so enthusiastically about your meetings and you were quite clearly kindred spirits, just as I would have expected. He told me how much fun you had been and how he loved your unusual sense of humour. He also told me quite a lot about Alice's numerous accomplishments, including many of her literary ones. I was astounded to hear that she had studied geology in her youth and even written a bit about it! You, with your so very wide interests, obviously couldn't have made a better match, and dear Kenneth, I know, would sympathise as much as me over your great loss.

Joyce's death, on the other hand, has been and still is even more difficult for me to come to terms with. She was all that John and I had left in a sense, and I in particular was no doubt over-dependent on her. John at least has always had his work to occupy his mind, while I, though I'm rather ashamed to admit this to you, have pretty much abandoned my 'career' – if ever I had one. When the children were small it was hard to find time to practise, and of course once one lets the practice go it is – as you must understand well – difficult to get back to one's former standard. And, as you would also appreciate, anything less than one's former standard is far from satisfactory. As the children got older, John, although not having strong musical inclinations himself, sometimes suggested that I take up teaching again, but the fact that his job caused us to make several moves around the country would have made that difficult even if I had felt up to it.

Then after Kenneth's death I didn't feel up to *anything* for quite a while, and no sooner had I *begun* to recover a little bit from that, when I was knocked for six by the loss of my daughter. I sometimes wish she had married, but on the other hand if she had had children who were soon to become semi-orphans that would not have been desirable either. It would have been lovely in a way to have had grandchildren, but I wouldn't have been of much use to them either as a grandmother or a substitute mother. I certainly feel too old for the latter!

In the matter of losing children, I am of course in good company: poor Dvorak, for instance, whom you so admire, lost his first *three* in less than three years! Harry's death from scarlet fever made you the eldest boy in your family, and the loss of your little brother Joe at only six must have been the most terrible blow, especially since you'd all regarded him as "the Beethoven of the family". When I listen to Dvorák's *Stabat Mater*, which I have done several times recently, I find it very easy to sense his intense grief at the death of his beloved daughter, and that is helpful to me in a strange sort of way. He was always sustained by his Roman Catholic faith, and I too have never lost my own faith in God, even though our, Unitarian, way of expressing that is so different from Dvorák's and yours. As you know, we are much less rigid in our beliefs, and different opinions are welcomed in our Church. Dvorák and his wife, though, did at least have more children later, while that has obviously long been precluded to me.

This letter is full of woe, which isn't really the *only* thing that I'd like to convey to you. For of course, besides having a loving husband and a good circle of loyal friends, music is still the most important thing in my life besides Kenneth and Joyce. It will ever be a constant source of consolation. Nowadays we don't have as many opportunities for concert going as I would like, but thank God for the wireless and my beloved gramophone! Thank God too that I still occasionally keep in touch with you through your music. I wrote ecstatically before about those absolutely wonderful *Variations* (in which I still hope – dare I say believe? – that I figure), yet now I feel that if one work of yours could be ranked as even more wonderful it would have to be the *Dream of Gerontius*. For years I felt that nothing could ever quite equal Dido's *Lament* for depth of beauty and poignancy over death, but then I heard your angel and I was completely transported to another world. When Kenneth died it was difficult for me and my family to keep our faith in God, but for me, when it wavered, I only needed to put on the wireless and, if they were playing, for instance, a Beethoven quartet, *anything* of Bach, or something of yours such as the *Introduction and Allegro* or the *Serenade* for Strings, my faith in something 'better' awaiting me would be instantly restored.

When I realised that Joyce was afflicted with consumption, first of all my memories of Mary Mercy's painful death, which was so *very* painful for both of us, came flooding back, and the shock and grief were unbearable. Then for a while I refused to believe how serious it was. I thought that, after all, since I had recovered from the disease after emigrating here, she surely could. As the doctors gradually became more and more pessimistic, I couldn't face the pain that the loss of our remaining child would bring, and so I locked it away in the basement and carried on performing my motherly and wifely duties just as usual. But then, when she passed away on 6 October 1921, the zombie that I had become simply crumbled and ceased to function. Someone removed the plug from the basin and all the water drained away in seconds. But, as I was lying in bed exhausted, my good friend Rosalind, who is an excellent viola player, came to visit, bringing with her her new records of *Gerontius*. She put them on in the correct order and slowly the tap was turned on and the water gradually, gradually began to refill the basin. By the time the angel started singing

"Softly and gently, dearly ransomed soul,

In my most loving arms I now enfold thee
And o'er the penal waters, as they roll,
I poise thee, and I lower thee, and hold thee..."
it was almost overflowing. Then, before anyone had time to turn
the tap off again, the water did overflow and at last my tears
came. They didn't stop for about three days, and then I felt
completely drained again and could scarcely move. John did his
level best to cope, keeping the stiff upper lip that his Scottish
ancestry had instilled in him, but he too of course was crippled
with pain deep inside and was also suffering badly from a gastric
ulcer.

During those next few weeks it was mainly Rosalind who
sustained us both; she kept us together really. Having herself lost
a child in infancy, she could empathise better than anyone else
we knew, and she also always sensed exactly which record
would suit me best at any given moment. Sometimes she would
lull me almost, or even completely, to sleep with the slow
movement of *the* Double Violin concerto, at other times she
would rouse me with one of the jolliest of J.S.'s cantatas and,
when she saw that my tears needed to flow again, she would put
on the *Siegfried Idyll*. How wonderful it must have been for
Wagner's wife Cosima when that work was first performed on
the stairs outside her bedroom as a gift for the birth of their son!
Hearing it of course always brought back instant memories of
my own children's births, which was painful, but Rosalind used
the memories as a trigger gently to get me to talk about some of
the joys that the two of them had brought me, of all the things
that we had shared together as a family, and then she would
remind us both that these were treasures that no one could ever
take away from us.

Now I don't know how much longer I shall have on this Earth
– often these days I am again afflicted with appalling bouts of
coughing – but when my time comes near, John, if he is still alive,
or alternatively one of my friends, will know to put *Gerontius* on

by my bedside. There *has* to be something better than this on the other side; how I hope you still believe that too! And who would I want more to transport me there than Gerontius' angel?

Your ever loving, if distressed,

Helen

Nervous, sensitive and kind,
Displays no vulgar frame of mind.
Ann Elgar writing of her son Edward

8 January 1928

Dearest Edward,

Well, I've finally made it! After writing my last Earthly letter to you, I lingered on for about another two and a half years. It was not an easy time, to put it mildly, and I did not even have the strength to go into Auckland for concerts. I moved back there first with Joyce when we'd realised how ill she was, as the climate in that area was deemed to be more favourable to her health than that of Hastings, and then, after her death in 1921 and John's retirement in 1922, the two of us moved together to Remuera, another suburb of Auckland. However, John's health was failing increasingly and, after his ulcer finally burst, he had a very painful death on 14 September 1925. He was buried, with Joyce of course, in Waikumete cemetery.

I am sure you can imagine how hard it was for me since I, like you, have always been such a people lover as well as an animal one, suddenly to be left with no family at all! Even my beloved cat died very soon after Joyce had, and it took me a long time to be persuaded to replace her. I was very fortunate still to have a good circle of friends. To beloved Bertha I bequeathed my precious gramophone and all my records, and to dear Brenda my sheet music and all the books that I had not already given to

Nelson College in memory of Kenneth. Rosalind, of whom I wrote before, had sadly already died not long before me. With these three great friends and others who had been such a wonderful support when we lost Joyce, I met regularly, normally in each other's houses. We always had plenty to talk about including music, and we often listened to music together even though our tastes varied somewhat. Once or twice they even persuaded me to take the old violin out of her case and I had a bash at playing your wonderful sonata, though not, I regret to say, with great success.

But after discovering in 1927 that, in addition to my weak lungs, I had a cancerous intestinal tumour, I thought it best to move to somewhere where I could be given full time care. Again I was fortunate since John had always been deservedly well paid for his hard work and so I wasn't short of money, and the Sisters of Mercy had a good reputation for the care they gave in Mater Misercordiae Hospital, Mount Eden. That is another suburb of Auckland and so my friends were still able to visit me right up until the last moments, just four days before my sixty-seventh birthday. I was given a beautiful funeral service and my ashes joined John and Joyce's grave on Christmas day last. And – need I say it! – the good nuns, being Catholic, were only too happy to facilitate my listening to *Gerontius* as I lay on my death bed.

So now that I have passed into spirit I needn't worry any longer about posting or not posting my letters to you! I can simply whisper what I want to tell you straight into your ear. Whether or not you think you hear me doesn't matter in the least because now I understand that it will all reach you on one level or another. Besides, although you won't realise it during the time when you are awake, souls on Earth normally leave their bodies when they are asleep at night, and at these times you sometimes meet me. We have already had one or two really good natters about our lives' purposes, and I look forward to more discussions with you before your time comes to join me over here.

In the meantime you may well be desirous of learning something about life in this realm, so I will now tell you a little bit about my personal experiences. Although the cancer caused me great pain for some months and I was appallingly weak physically, once I had realised that my end was nigh, I somehow gained in strength mentally. I prayed a lot, pleading with the Lord to take me easily as well as to look after the world that I felt ready to leave, and I prepared myself well, writing out a detailed will just three months before my departure. Since I no longer felt close to any of my own family back in England, my chief beneficiaries were John's two unmarried sisters, who had always been good to me. Upon their deaths all remaining capital from our, now my, estate was to be divided equally between the orphanages of Auckland and the vicinity. Well, I knew only too well what it was like to be orphaned, and of course the children in those homes have lost their parents much earlier than I did. Also, I'm sure you will be glad to hear that I bequeathed £50 to the Auckland Society for Prevention of Cruelty to Animals.

As December 1927 wore on I began gently to detach myself from my wasting physical body that was so racked with pain. I floated in and out for a while, often aware of angelic presences surrounding me, ever attentive to my needs, and at times I was even able to converse with John, Kenneth and Joyce. So, when my day finally arrived and I had said all my "goodbyes", I simply floated away from Earth, aided – I repeat! – by Gerontius' angel quite literally taking me into his arms just at *that* moment in the music. So, dear Edward, please take my word for it: death need hold no fear at all for anyone.

Once I had looked back down and saw my physical body lying on the bed, I gradually became aware that the angel with the so wonderful voice had become my own guardian angel, who has been with me since the beginning of time. He (or was it she?) carried me to a boat which was moored at the edge of the most beautiful river I have ever seen. And who was in the boat but my dear husband John! We were overjoyed to see one another and he told me straight away that Kenneth and Joyce were waiting for us on the other side of the river. In what seemed like no time at all I was clambering – or rather drifting – out of the boat, holding tight to John's hand, and there indeed were my two darling children waiting to embrace me. They said, "You see now how partings are never for ever," and that they would in due course be able to explain to me the reasons why they had both had such short lives. They said that it had been for the growth of all four of us, but that I needn't concern myself about that right now because I first needed to spend a bit of time in hospital to be given some healing. Listening to their words and embracing all three members of my close family, I suddenly knew deep down that everything was exactly as it was always meant to be and was quite perfect.

So here I am now in this incredibly beautiful etheric hospital and just coming to the end of my course of healing. At first I was so weary that all I wanted to do was sleep, but now I am awake all the time, learning things that are at the same time both new and not new. By which I mean that they seem new simply because I had forgotten; gradually each 'new' piece of information I am given strikes something deep inside me and I am now re-remembering more and more. Everything here is bewitchingly wonderful, and the treatment I am receiving is infinitely more effective than any medicine I ever experienced on Earth. It consists of colour and light therapy, massage from angels who use the most wonderful aromas I have ever smelt, and music that – believe it or not – is even more exquisite than the very best of either Johann Sebastian or your good self. I am feeling stronger every day, and shortly I shall be going to a Council meeting to decide upon the type of work best suited to me during the time that I shall have here before I am due for my next incarnation. Yes, dear, we do have lots and lots, whatever your Church may teach! How else could we learn all we need to learn and do all that we want to do? And on that happy note I will close for the time being.

    With lots of love from,

    Helen

Dearest Edward,

This letter has no date because now I am outside time. I cannot begin to tell you how wonderful it is being Home once again, and also being able to travel in no time at all more or less wherever I want to. I don't yet have a 'passport' to the very highest realms – that will come once I have returned to Earth possibly a few more times and worked off the remains of my karma – but, if there is someone I want to talk to, I only have to think of them in order to come instantly into their presence. I've met both of my birth parents, and of course my dear stepmother, and have been made to see that a large part of their tasks and also of my own family's was to help me to learn about loss. My guides assure me that I have now learnt that lesson well and will not therefore have to endure so much loss in a future incarnation. I've also seen a lot of John, Kenneth and Joyce and we've had some very happy times together, but firstly none of them is in my soul group and secondly they each have different work from mine over here. We are all busy now and, while enjoying the fact that we can meet up whenever we want, we no longer need to spend a lot of time together. My work, I trust you will be interested to hear, is helping people to cross over when it is their time – especially those who are suffering a lot from physical illness.

So you see, I am now mixing mainly with members of my own soul group, which is absolutely wonderful because we all know and understand one another perfectly. We never have arguments as everyone does at some time or another during their Earthly sojourns, we all understand one another's individual gifts, and we work together in perfect harmony without the slightest element of competition or 'one-upmanship'. Believe it or not, I have discovered – or rather rediscovered – that Johann Sebastian is a member of my soul group, and he has reminded me that I was the most devoted of his daughters during that incarnation. He admits, by the way, that I did have a tough time as the unmarried Johanna Carolina Bach, often working late into the night copying out manuscripts in extremely poor lighting, but we both know that I had taken it on willingly on account of my total devotion to the music. His and my mother's teaching me to play the lute in that lifetime stood me in good stead as Helen when I decided to take up the violin.

And guess who else I am seeing a lot of now, and who is also a member of my soul group: Alice! Yes, I mean *your* Alice – the one who stood by you through thick and thin and without whom you would probably never have achieved quite so much glory as a composer. We looked back together at the Plans we made for our most recent lives. At one point it was a tossup between which of us would marry you – I had been your wife in a fairly recent previous incarnation while she had previously been your mother in another one – but, aided by the advice of our guides, as well as you yourself, it soon became clear to all three of us that she would be the person best suited to your particular needs this time. She, we all believed, would have the stamina to weather your moodiness (a characteristic of so many of the world's greatest artists since it of course adds colour and greatness to your work), whereas I would have all too easily been got down by it. Besides, I very much wanted to have a musical career of my own, whereas she was more willing to sacrifice her own ends to yours. So you see, dear Edward, what happened for all three of us during the nineteenth to twentieth centuries was what had been intended and what was best for our learning and what we had planned to achieve, even though it entailed so much pain and grief. Grief and pain help us to grow, but one day, the Masters tell me, we shall learn to evolve through joy. Please remember that when you are feeling particularly down. Alice appreciates now that she wasn't an ideal mother – poor Carice was also made to suffer for the sake of your work and Alice often made her do things that she didn't enjoy at all – but Carice also needed to learn to stand on her own feet, and she will do a wonderful job of promoting you and your work after your death.

You know, I think one day, if I have a daughter again, I shall name her after Alice. She is such a good friend, I have so much admiration and respect for her, and anyway it is such a pretty name!

Your ever loving,

Helen

2 June 1930

"This is where two souls merge and melt into one another."
E.E whispered to Vera Hockman while listening to the recording of the fifteen-year old Yehudi Menuhin playing the Violin Concerto, and after he had lingered lovingly over the last melting phrases of the slow movement.

My dear Edward,

Looking back towards Earth, Alice and I, who, as I have told you previously are now outside time, can see that you are turning seventy-three. Your health, which has never been very good, is failing more and more, and before very much longer your life will be drawing to a close. What's more, another world war will shortly be brewing, and we both know only too well that that is something you will certainly wish to avoid. Anyway, HAPPY BIRTHDAY from us both, and may you and Carice and the dogs have a very enjoyable day together! At least the weather should be pleasant for you. By the way, Alice says that she's sorry that her aversion to dogs prevented you from having any all those years, but they would only have been yet another distraction from your important work. She is glad that you didn't lose too much time after her passing in making up for that long deprivation, even if getting five of them was a bit over the top!

However, before you prepare to depart the Earth, something very exciting and wonderful is going to befall you. You see from 'up here', for want of a better way of putting it, we have a very much broader perspective than you have. It is easy for us to look both into the distant past and into the future. In reality such terms are meaningless, but that is something which is impossible to understand while we are limited to an Earthly perspective. So, looking into the rather close 'future' we can see that you're soon going to be given the great joy of meeting your 'twin soul'. I need to explain. The phrase 'soul mates' is a fairly broad term covering different types of intimate and loving relationships. Had you and Alice been needing to pay a debt one to the other, you would have been 'karmic soul mates', but in fact she, like me, is one of your 'companion soul mates'. I made it clear in my last letter that we were all three old friends, and for that reason we are comfortable together, fall in love with each other easily, and are able to have fruitful relationships during our Earthly sojourns.

However, at the beginning, when every 'droplet of God' was working harmoniously with Him on the great work of Creation, each soul split into two to go their separate ways. That is why, while on Earth, most of us are always searching for our 'other half', whom we naturally see as the 'perfect mate', the one who will understand us totally as no other human being can. From time to time we do meet up on Earth, always for a good reason, whether the meeting brings intense joy or intense pain. 'Twin soul' relationships are invariably huge learning experiences. Your twin soul's name is Vera and, though she is considerably younger than you and you are not destined to marry in your present lives, you will quickly recognise each other and become extremely close. She, like me, is a violinist, and you will probably meet when she is playing in our beloved *Gerontius* when you are conducting it. Alice and I will be watching it all unfold, as well as continuing with our own individual work, and it will give us great joy to see you finally finding the 'perfect love' for which you have been searching for so long. She will be the muse that you have been needing ever since you were widowed, and we hope that she will inspire a good deal more of that wonderful music.

Some people may find it hard to understand your 'infatuation' with a younger woman, but you can ignore that because bodily physical age is meaningless. It is only the soul that really counts, and you and Vera have always belonged to one another and always will. We don't meet with our twin soul in every incarnation – far from it – but when we do it is for a specific purpose. Her purpose this time will be, as I just said, to provide you with new inspiration for your work, that having dried up somewhat since your dear Alice's death. Don't worry too much, however, if you're unable to complete everything you have in mind before departing from Earth. Pressure may well be put on you for, for instance, a third symphony, but you will have to look after yourself first. It will always be possible for someone else to do something with your snippets after you have returned here, in which case you will be able to oversee it from the world of spirit. Even if, when you are at the end of your life and demand that nothing be done with your symphony snippets – or even ask for them to be burnt – once you have crossed over and are able to see things from a higher perspective, I'm sure that you will change your mind.

And once you are back here, you will be able to read your own *Akashic Records*. Everything that we have ever done since the beginning of time is recorded in the ether – it is that that enables clairvoyants on Earth to make past life readings for people – and once you have looked at yours, you will see how often you have been a skilled musician in the past. Your family couldn't afford to send you to a music college, but in reality you didn't need that because all that you needed to know about composition, as well as about playing different instruments, was stored in your subconscious. It only needed practice for your innate abilities to shine forth and enable you to produce works of music even greater than any that you had produced before in previous lives. That took work of course, and part of the work that was needed also involved your struggle to overcome what prejudiced people saw as an 'inauspicious background'. Fortunately you had family and friends all along the way who saw your potential and encouraged you to realise it, but mainly getting where you have has been your own doing. Meeting Vera will be your end of life reward for all the obstacles that you have overcome, and together you will produce great things even if the world fails to recognise them straight away.

Your religion has for some years now been only nominal. Your refusal to accompany Alice to Sunday mass grieved her at the time; she converted to Catholicism just when your own faith was failing and thereafter took it very seriously. As for Carice, whom Alice dutifully had brought up as Catholic, she will never waver from Catholicism. However, now that Alice is over here she has a much broader perspective of spiritual matters and she understands that your *real* spirituality had nothing to do with the Church of your upbringing and a lot more to do with the natural world around you. If on your deathbed you upset anyone by refusing to see a priest, it won't matter at all in the broader picture. Isn't *Gerontius* sufficient requiem for you? I know that you wrote of it to your great friend Jaeger: "I'm truly glad you like the thing cos I've written it out of my insidest inside." Well, many people are too afraid to express their "insidest inside"! The fact that you were not afraid to do so is one of the many things that have made you truly great, and it is also why so many people, including myself of course, have been so intensely moved by that particular work.

It will be hard for Vera when you depart, but again that loss will be an important part of her learning and you will reunite when it is her turn to cross over. I myself have found much ecstasy over here in being able to meet up with my own twin, but he is now due to reincarnate shortly before your departure from Earth and I don't yet know when we shall reunite. It might not be on Earth again, but that won't matter because it is only on a much higher plane, and when we are ready to make our final return to Source, that Sun and Moon can once more fuse in perfect ecstasy. So, until EE's work on Earth is done, Alice and I wish you and Vera many happy times together.

Love and blessings,

Helen

PART THREE

HELEN AND ANN

CHAPTER ONE

Reflections

The great lesson in life is: become what you are.
Maureen Lipman (talking to Sarah Walker on Radio 3 on 19
June 2013)

Talking in an interview about his realisation of Elgar's third symphony, the composer Anthony Payne said that he had felt EE "on his shoulder" all the time that he was working at it. (Please forgive me if I have mis-remembered AP's words a little bit, but that was certainly the gist of what he said.) Well, I personally believe that a hundred per cent. Apparently during his final years, when he was battling with cancer at the same time as endeavouring to honour his contract with the BBC for a third symphony, EE said that he did not want anyone else to complete the work for him. However, as I hope I already made clear in Helen's post-death letters, once we cross over and are able to look back to Earth and at our last life and its achievements, we gain a much broader and higher perspective. That being the case, I would be amazed if Elgar in spirit would have wanted his marvellous sketches to remain hidden rather than being recorded for all to hear. The most obvious way to do this was surely for the jigsaw to be completed by someone competent to do so, and EE, from his elevated position on the other side, was no doubt also the best person to make the selection of composer. Unqualified as I may be in matters musical, I am full of admiration for Payne's rendering of Elgar's presumed intentions. The mammothness of his task can be surmised by what Michael Kennedy said in his masterly book: "What remains of Elgar's third symphony amounts to sketches of a sketch for a sketch"! To me Payne's third EE symphony sounds no less Elgarian than either of the other two, and I rejoice in the fact that the wonderful snippets that were left behind by the fatally sick Elgar have now seen the light of day. I also feel sure that EE himself shares this joy with Ann and Helen!

I am making no such claims for myself. Although I too was most certainly feeling EE's spirit around me when the letters, which make up Part Two of this little book were writing themselves, I have no intention of claiming to have been channelling Elgar. That is not to say that I don't believe in channelling. Far from it: I am fully prepared to believe that Anthony Payne was actually channelling EE when he was weaving the left-behind snippets together into a complete symphony. Tony Neate, the internationally known Malvern therapist who founded the College of Healing jointly with his wife Ann and others from Runnings Park, has a book, *Channelling for Everyone*,[1] which I intend to study seriously when I can find the time. In the meantime, though, I hope that I already made it quite clear in my Introduction that I regarded EE's style as inimitable and that I was consequently expressing what I *felt* were his feelings and sometimes simply having a bit of fun on his behalf. (After all, he was such a fun lover [*and* giver!] when he wasn't in one of his 'black moods' [Helen] or 'mouldy' [Alice]!)

When it comes to Helen Weaver, however, it is a totally different matter, since both in the regression that I did in 2012, and in my subsequent reflections, I genuinely believe myself to have been feeling her feelings. However, by stating too that I believe myself to be the same soul reincarnated it is not my intention to make a claim to fame. If one or more people were, after reading this book, to say to me, "You can't possibly have been Helen W because *I* was!" it wouldn't bother me in the slightest. For one thing I would be no more able to prove them wrong than to prove myself right. For another, again as I explained in the Introduction, we DMP therapists have no interest in proving anything; our only interest is in healing. So I shall come to the healing as my Conclusion, but first of all I will list my own reasons for believing the discovery that came to me so unexpectedly in 2012, together with a few comments about the similarities and differences between Helen and myself now as Ann. If our personalities were identical each time round, we wouldn't achieve our necessary learning. However, as I hope I have already made clear, whether or not I the author am or am not actually the same soul as Helen Weaver is *not* the main point of this book. Readers can all draw your own conclusions according to your own belief systems.

The most obvious similarity is a shared love of music that dated from an early age, but jointly with that goes the startling difference between our abilities on the violin. My lack of musical talent first bothered me for years and years and then, after I had come to learn about reincarnation and discovered that I *had* had that talent in previous lives, it puzzled me. I already said that I don't like mysteries – I get irritated by novels or films that end with a question mark about what happens next – and so I determined to get an answer on this matter. In the shamanic soul rescue work that I do, I use a drumming CD acquired from the Sacred Trust, with whom I completed two training weekends. This drumming helps one to relax and provides a good escort into other realms, where one can meet with, for instance, spirit guides, of whom we all normally have about three or four, and obtain answers to questions that are on our mind. So, when one day I asked, "Whoever is up there who can give me an answer," the reason for my not having brought musical talent into my present life, a response came into my head instantly and with crystalline clarity. They (whoever "they" were, and that matters to me not at all) said, "It's because, if you had been talented at it, you would have wanted to make music your career, and that's not what you agreed to this time round."

Problem solved – and totally to my satisfaction since it was so obviously true! In fact, when I went to the 2011 *'Mouliners'* meeting in France (the year before my big discovery about HW), I was having difficulty in getting my third book accepted for publication and feeling sorely tempted to chuck it all in and retire into grandmotherhood. My colleagues' response on that occasion was "Right, let's get you into your Life Plan." They took me back to pre-conception, when I was discussing my aims and purpose for this lifetime as Ann, and I saw myself quite clearly "signing a contract" to get all these books out, despite being warned about it entailing "big challenges and difficulties". (I also, thanks to Marion suggesting it, met a new spirit guide who was coming in to help me make amendments to my book on the Life Plan and then get it published, and he was indeed successful.) So now I no longer envy people who are good at playing musical instruments, but instead endeavour to carry on working at improving and completing my writing (at the same time as enjoying grandmotherhood!).

A second important point is that of religion and spirituality. It is generally accepted that EE's Catholicism was a stumbling block for Helen, who was a Unitarian. Besides not believing in the Trinity, Unitarians are very much more open-minded than the majority of Christians and actually welcome different viewpoints rather than having a strict code of beliefs to which all their members are expected to adhere. I was very strictly Catholic for the greater part of this, my present life, as well as having been a nun in numerous previous lives, but I am also certain that I was a Cathar at the time of the Albigensian Crusade (1209–29). Nowadays, with my interest in Indian spirituality (an interest shared incidentally by Gustav Holst), my Christianity leans much more towards Catharism. Even more importantly, I now believe that there are as many paths up the spiritual mountain as there are people to climb it and rejoice in the fact that all three of my children are busy finding their own way, which in each case is as far away from Catholicism as it is to my own present form of spirituality. I have therefore in this lifetime moved from EE's denomination towards Helen's. It is also my personal belief that EE himself – at least towards the end of his life – was no longer hidebound by Catholicism but inclined to a more spiritual direction. Latterly, as Helen 'wrote', he no longer attended mass every Sunday, which in Catholicism is regarded much more than in other Churches as a heinous crime.

The next important issue is health. There is much uncertainty over Helen's reasons for breaking off her engagement and going to New Zealand, and this uncertainty includes a question mark as to whether she did or did not have TB like the stepmother she had cared for when she was dying. Following my regression, in which my chest played an involuntary but key role, I am convinced (with Cora Weaver) that she did indeed have TB, though quite how serious it was I have no way of telling. She recovered of course, sufficiently well to marry and have two children, but I'm quite sure that her Worcester family thought her sickness grave enough to merit her move to warmer climes. (In the regression I 'heard' talk of Australia before the aunt in Auckland came up with her kind offer of hospitality.)

We come to each of our many lives with different lessons to learn, different things to do, different debts to pay, different acquaintances to make or renew. This of course makes for variety, which in turn leads to the formation of all-rounded characters. Some things, however, do get repeated for good reason (for instance my own intense love of music), while others get repeated for less good reasons. Often we get trapped into a pattern (for instance someone who repeatedly falls in love with the same man, who every time abuses her). Often a physical deformity or malady is stored in the subconscious and then is unwittingly imprinted onto the new body. This is where a therapy such as the one I practise can be uniquely useful, because bringing a subconscious issue into the conscious mind enables us to let go of it and move on.

Well I, thank goodness, have never had TB, but my lungs are

nevertheless one of my weakest organs. We moved to Shropshire partly for the hill walking, which is still one of our favourite pastimes, but I am always extremely slow on the up bits and get breathless very easily. At school the principal thing that my five friends and I had in common was a dislike of sport, and I have *never* been able to run, which again is mainly a lung problem. So I now believe that weakness to be one of Helen's legacies, which doesn't, however, mean making no attempt to overcome it. Mounting Caer Caradoc (another version of the name 'Caractacus'!) for a third time is a current ambition.

On the plus side, we come each time, as I just said, to learn particular lessons. In therapy sessions, after the client has been through a death into the *Bardo* and is being helped to review the life that has ended, the questions we ask are, "What was your main purpose? Did you achieve it? What had you come to learn? Do you feel that you did learn that lesson well or not?" and so on. Sometimes one of the lessons we choose is to learn to cope with loss, and that was surely one that Helen Weaver had chosen! In the letter that she wrote on EE's birthday in 1924, she spoke eloquently of all her tragic losses. I, on the other hand – apart from suffering the devastatingly early deaths of a couple of dogs, the fact that one of my school friends died of cancer when she was only fifty-five, and that both Sai Baba and Roger Woolger died in 2011 – have to date been fortunate in never yet having experienced any really serious personal losses. This to me indicates that Helen learnt her lesson well and is now being rewarded for it. She lost both her children before they had reached the age of thirty, while I now have three children who are all in their thirties. Furthermore, I am at present blessed with three delightful young grandchildren – a thing that Helen would no doubt have loved to have experienced.

Travel to different countries is another important point. In certain lifetimes we get strongly drawn to visit places where we have something karmic to deal with, places of which we still have, all be it subconsciously, happy memories, or places where we need to do some healing, either for ourselves or for one or more of our ancestors. So many people are drawn, for instance, to the war graves of Normandy. And my family no doubt all have happy memories of Geneva! Well, in 2010 a financial policy that we had taken out ten years previously came to fruition. I said to David, who fortunately agreed, "This will enable us to keep my long-held promise to visit my cousin Charles in Australia." I was genuinely keen to do that, but I wanted even more to go to New Zealand, and it seemed logical to 'do Down Under' in one fell swoop (especially since we had no further policies incubating!). So we had the good fortune of escaping most of that dreadful winter of 2010–11 and, what's more, we had a really wonderful time. Charles and Margaret in Canberra looked after us superbly, I enjoyed seeing Sydney, which my mother had talked about so much throughout my childhood, we sailed the Whitsunday Islands and then went up to Cairns and saw the Great Barrier Reef as well as travelling both through and over (in a cable car) the rain forest to a fascinating Aboriginal village. Then after all that we flew to – yes, you've guessed it! – Auckland.

Since I'm now the only driver, I decided when planning this big trip that, rather than hiring a car or a mobile home as do so many visitors to New Zealand, I would prefer to do an organised tour. We had the previous summer immensely enjoyed a Schubertiade with ACE Cultural Tours, and in their brochure I found a 'Nature Quest tour' of New Zealand which sounded wonderful and whose dates suited our itinerary perfectly. So I booked that and asked ACE at the same time to book us some extra days in Auckland both before and after the tour. This was partly because we had some friends we had made in Sai Baba's ashram, who lived near Auckland, and we were keen to meet them again. I did not of course at that time yet know consciously about having previously been Helen Weaver; I only knew *subconsciously* that Auckland was somewhere I was keen to see again. I could after all have asked ACE to book us, for instance, some extra time in Dunedin, where the tour actually started, but no, Auckland was my unhesitating choice.

Had we made the trip a couple of years later, after making my big discovery and reading Cora Weaver's book, I would certainly have endeavoured to visit at least one or two of the spots she mentions as being places where Helen lived. Were I ever to have another opportunity to go to New Zealand I would certainly do that, as well as looking for the Munro family grave, but I don't feel that it matters too much. All that really matters to me is understanding why I had had such a strong yen to visit that country. Helen never quite got over her EE heartbreak, and she did miss Worcestershire, but she made New Zealand her home and developed a great love for it. A love which, now that I've seen quite a lot of this amazing country, I fully understand.

Another thing that I feel Helen and myself to have in common is a strong spirit of independence. In the nineteenth century much more than in our day it must have been a very big thing for a young woman to go to the other side of the globe entirely on her own. Her health was poor, she had never met the family who were initially offering her hospitality and she can't have had much of an idea of what to expect there, yet she took the plunge with the idea of making herself a completely new home. Even going off to study in Leipzig prior to that must have been quite a big step for a young Worcester shoe shop proprietor's daughter! I've never been as far as New Zealand on my own, and Geneva, where I settled alone at the age of twenty-nine, is of course much less far, but I was only seventeen when I first went off to Spain for a summer 'au pair' job. Besides, firstly my homoeopath has always said that I have "a weak constitution but a strong will", and secondly, doing the work that I do nowadays, which is often subject to scepticism or even derision, takes a good deal of determination, as does getting books published.

Now for some minor points. Firstly, I was surprised when I

read that Helen's children were called Kenneth and Joyce because I've never liked either of those names. Could this be because they had such sad connotations for me? On the other hand, I've always liked the name Helen, and is it pure coincidence that my own name is Ann, with the (slightly less common) spelling as EE's mother? On a completely different front, Elgar's five foot ten would have made him seem tall in the nineteenth century, and I have always had a bit of a 'thing' about tall men. Finally, David when I first met him had a ginger moustache (which matched his then ginger hair). Thinking that it didn't suit him, I persuaded him when we first started going out together to shave it off. Now, looking in the photos at EE's extremely prominent moustache, I can't help wondering whether David's was the "wrong colour" for me, or whether again men with moustaches had sad connotations for me!

Sadly there seem to be no extant photographs of Helen, but I believe that she was pretty. (Michael Kennedy quotes Elgar writing: "The pretty lady is on the sea and far away.") Though it no longer matters to me since my husband has always found me attractive, I have never been pretty. (In our family it was rubbed in over and over that Philippa was the pretty one!) Obviously each new body that we take on has a different appearance from previous ones and, that being the case, people sometimes wonder how it is possible in regressions to recognise people that one has known before. The answer seems to be – and this is also my personal experience – that the way to do it is by looking into their eyes. After all, the eyes are always said, are they not, to be the window of the soul?

Over and above all these points, however, my main reason for now believing myself to have previously been Helen Weaver is quite simply that it explains the feelings I have had for and about Sir Edward Elgar ever since I first came to know of his existence in about 1956. Also, the first time that I read about Helen Weaver, something 'lit up' in my head and now in retrospect I can see that

I was subsequently always on the lookout for more information about her. Furthermore, as I mentioned in the first chapter of this book, the moment that I first fell in love with EE's music and started reading about him, I felt as though I had always known him. That has never changed and I'm sure that it never will!

Note

1. *CHANNELLING FOR EVERYONE – A safe, step-by-step guide to developing your intuition and psychic awareness*, Tony Neate, Piatkus, 1997.

CHAPTER TWO

Healing

Bach challenges us to BE BETTER!
Sir Nicholas Kenyon

In one of his inspiring talks given on the 2013 Martin Randall J. S. Bach Journey, Sir Nicholas Kenyon quoted Malcolm Gladwell's[1] claim that genius was the fruit of both genes and circumstances. I dispute neither of these – still less do I dispute Gladwell's argument in one of his earlier books[2] that instinctive first thoughts and impressions can always be relied upon – but my question for the sceptics is: are genes and circumstances really *enough* to explain the absolutely outstanding abilities of, say, J.S.B or EE – not to mention Mozart, Beethoven, Shakespeare or many other of the world's greatest names? Gladwell says, "Superstar lawyers and math whizzes and software entrepreneurs appear at first blush to lie outside ordinary experience." He doesn't mention musicians here, but would no doubt include them. He continues, "But they don't. They are products of history and community, or opportunity and legacy." With these four I agree, but I agree much less when he goes on to say that "Their success is not exceptional or mysterious." How could anyone deny Bach or Shakespeare the label of "exceptional"? Gladwell's conclusion about genius is that "It is grounded in a web of advantages and inheritances, some deserved, some not, some earned, some just plain lucky – but all critical to making them who they are." Without disputing this list, I would substitute "karma and previous experience" for the phrase "plain lucky", and I do not personally care for the word 'outlier'; my dictionary does recognise it as a word, but not in the sense that Gladwell is clearly giving it. Why not call such people "exceptional" or simply stick to the word 'genius'?

Johann Sebastian was of course born into history's largest and most renowned musical dynasty, but he was orphaned at the age of ten. His musical father, Ambrosius Bach, taught him before he died, and then the boy went to live with his older half-brother, Johann Christoph, who continued the teaching. However, neither of these two, gifted though they no doubt were, has gone down in history as an important composer; nor do musicologists put even the most talented of the next generation – Wilhelm Friedemann, Carl Philip Emmanuel and Johann Christian – into the same league as their father for composition. Johann Sebastian had no formal higher education at all, and neither did Elgar. We really have to say that both J.S. Bach and EE were basically entirely self-taught. The latter's father was a piano tuner by profession and also an enthusiastic musician, but he came nowhere near to approaching his son's gifts. Michael Kennedy (referring in this instance to Elgar's symphonies) says that "the ingenuity, whether conscious or sub-conscious, is of a kind that only a composer of the highest, Beethovenian, calibre commands." And of the *Enigma Variations* he says in the same book, "It is, in my opinion, the greatest orchestral work yet written by an Englishman." Also, George Bernard Shaw, writing in the first issue of 'Music and Letters', said that Elgar was "carrying on Beethoven's business."

After the Polish pianist, composer and politician Paderewski was asked where Elgar had studied and he replied, "Nowhere," the next question was "Who taught him?" to which the reply was *"Le Bon Dieu."* Well, I believe in a Good God as strongly as anybody could, but why should He choose to teach composition only to a select few? Doesn't the notion of we ourselves having chosen a certain métier in which to specialise, and then to improve our expertise by practising it repeatedly, make a lot more sense? And, if we accept this (N.B. very widespread and in the Western world ever-increasing) belief, doesn't it further make perfect sense that a potential great composer should choose to be born into a musical family, for encouragement as well as for the genes?

If I were told that I was only allowed to have the music of one composer on my desert island, I would have to insist on two: Elgar and Bach. Even that would be difficult because how could I survive for long without the Beethoven quartets and cello sonatas, some Schubert *Lieder*, and at least a few little bits of, for instance, Purcell, Monteverdi, Mozart or Brahms? (Unlike my "beloved", I could live very easily without Wagner!) Fortunately no desert island is at present in sight and, now that we have paid off our mortgage, David and I are fortunate to be able to go on adding to our CD collection as well as attend concerts regularly and even treat ourselves to the occasional musical holiday. (For these we have been very happy with both Martin Randall Travel and ACE Cultural Tours).

So why, out of all these great loves, do I put Bach and Elgar – two such strongly contrasting composers – right at the top? Some of my colleagues would say that it was "because of your past life connections with those two composers", but here for a moment I want to talk purely about their music. Others infinitely more competent than I am have already done this very comprehensively (for EE I strongly recommend both Michael Kennedy and Diana McVeagh, and for Bach Sir Nicholas Kenyon[3] and Christoph Wolf[4] are both invaluable), so what I have to say, very briefly, is a purely personal, and totally non-expert, viewpoint.

Although I am confident of still having a number of years to go (hopefully enough to finish all my books!), I can no longer avoid facing the fact of being on the last lap. And for me that fact – and its inevitable consequence of looking towards what may lie ahead – results in my putting the spiritual side of life first. Less and less these days do I like big cities, crowds and noise, and more and more do I feel intense disgust at vandalism, litter, drug abuse, alcoholism and the other negative aspects of life on Earth.

Sai Baba and all the other Masters encourage being "in the world but not of it". When it comes to attaining spirituality everyone has their own preferred method; for some it is church going, for others meditation, some find it best through nature, others – like myself – are moved in that direction even more by music. William Bloom, who is at present generally regarded as this country's leading writer on spirituality, talks in his most recent, highly acclaimed, book[5] about the importance of music. He says,

> From Christian hymns and classical music, through gongs and tribal drums to rock concerts, it is well understood that music and rhythm, especially if experienced over a long period of time and in a heartfelt way, will take most people into an altered state of consciousness and a sense of spiritual connection. Hearts open. Minds calm down...

For me, of all the greatest composers, J. S. Bach, being according to my school of thought a highly evolved soul, is the one who was the most pure channel for the divine. EE himself once wrote to his friend Ivor Atkins, "Bach heals and pacifies all men and all things" and, after Alice's death, he depended on people like Bach for inspiration. Sir Nicholas Kenyon said in one of his above-mentioned talks that Bach worked constantly and endlessly to improve upon his compositions, and I have no reason to doubt this. I, however, have never heard a work of his that seemed to my comparatively 'unmusical' ear to be anything less than perfect and, were I ever to lose faith in God or in eternal life, it would be to Bach's music that I would turn to get it restored. The very title of Sir John Eliot Gardiner's forthcoming book – *Music in the Castle of Heaven* – describes my feelings precisely. For how could anything so wonderful as Bach's music have come from this, so very imperfect, world?

Whether it be Bach or another composer who is their particular favourite, I feel sure that musical atheists and agnostics share these feelings in their own way, and that they have their personal equivalents for the word 'divine'. Sir Nicholas Kenyon echoed my own thoughts about Bach's relationship with the divine when he said in one of his talks to the 2013 Martin Randall 'J.S. Bach pilgrims' that, since he saw God in everything, God permeated Bach's secular works just as much as they did the sacred ones.

The Third Programme (and I think Radio 3 as well) for very many years always played Bach cantatas on Sunday mornings. When I was at university and living at home (a thing I would not recommend to anyone if they can help it!), my mother, younger siblings and I would come home from mass each Sunday morning and I would promptly put on the wireless so as not to miss the cantatas while we were having breakfast. My father invariably complained! I suppose I was lucky that he didn't make me switch the wireless off, but perhaps he was thereby showing some deference to my mother. Well, since Radio 3 can no longer be relied upon for these cantatas every Sunday, I decided a few years ago to reinstate them myself. We haven't yet acquired the whole John Eliot Gardiner twenty-eight volume set, but are reasonably well on the way to it. Far from complaining, David enjoys them as much as I do and, since neither of us now has a church we wish to attend, this has become our joint way of making Sunday breakfast special. For me the cantatas are a seemingly bottomless goldmine; their numerousness of course helps that, but they are also ever fresh however many times one hears them.

EE, on the other hand, has greater variety in his works, and by no means all of them reach anything like Bach's perfection. Yet, if it is spirituality I am seeking, it is to be found there too. Surpassedly, for me at any rate, in *Gerontius*, but so many of EE's masterpieces have either smaller or bigger flashes of deep spirituality also. But while Bach to my mind speaks mainly to the soul, intellect and heart, Elgar often goes right to the gut as well.

Ever a 'larger than life' personality, his music echoes that by covering the full gamut of human emotion and feeling. That is why I could never do without both of these great composers. While we are still in this world, we have to be in a body too, and being *in* the body also requires paying attention to it and its needs. William Bloom talks of the need to ground oneself in the body for full spiritual experience. (He also says that "Staying silent about what is important to you is not healthy. It is a form of repression and denial that can affect psychological and physical wellbeing." Hence this present book of mine!)

But now to return to my 2013 *'Mouliners'* meeting. Although I was at that juncture busily writing the EE–HW correspondence, more or less everything that I wanted to say was now clear in my mind and I felt that I had pretty much 'dealt with' Helen since the previous year's reunion. So I told my friends that what I wanted to find out this time was what it *felt* like being a daughter of Bach's. I had had on a Woolger workshop many years previously, when he was beginning the day's work with a little piece of Bach, a flashback picture of a little girl sitting on the floor listening to J.S. himself playing the harpsichord. I subsequently obtained confirmation of that lifetime as a member of the Bach family, but my homoeopath has always constantly encouraged me to get in touch with and express my feelings. In fact, ever since my little brush with cancer in 2012, he has been doing that even more on account of the fact that creative expression can be very therapeutic. (The positive effect of play therapy for disturbed children is well known. Often, for instance, they can be encouraged to express their feelings by using doll's house characters to speak for them.) In fact the frustration caused by unexpressed creativity is another possible contributory factor in the onset of something such as cancer, and so it seemed to me now to be very important to get on with my writing as well as taking Essiac, which is a herbal remedy renowned for cancer prevention as well as cure.

I had tried in vain on my own to get into Johanna Carolina Bach's feelings, and knew that my friends' assistance would help greatly with that, which indeed it did. So now I have another question for the sceptics: before doing the regression I knew nothing about Johanna Carolina other than her name and the fact that she was the daughter of Anna Magdalena Bach, not Maria Barbara. In the regression I saw that her older sister got married while she did not, and I saw her not only playing the lute in a family group but also copying out music and – later, after her father had died – working hard at putting together and cataloguing some of these great works for the benefit of posterity. Well, hanging on the wall in the Leipzig Bach Museum is a family tree and when, six weeks after my Mouliners' meeting in France, I visited Leipzig for the first time on the J.S. Bach Journey, I read there that "From 1753 Johanna Carolina Bach took on writing tasks for the family." The family tree also confirmed the marital statuses that I had seen of the two sisters. How can anyone who refuses to accept my lifetime as Johanna Carolina as a fact explain that?

When I had the floor at the meeting, I told my colleagues that, before exploring JCB, I would like to read them one of the Elgar letters that they had seen me scrawling so busily. I chose the one containing the comparison of EE with Purcell, which I had just completed, and they all enjoyed it. I had actually wanted to write a letter in response to an article in the Elgar Society Journal discussing this matter but, having never found the time to get round to it, had now enjoyed allowing EE to do it for me! Then, after the end of my session, we had some further discussion, and the unanimous opinion was that I would do better to make the HW and EE topic a little book all on its own – especially since I had expressed a desire for my book to be sold at profit to the Elgar Birthplace Museum.

Thinking about the Bach lifetime I had just been exploring, plus several others that I still had in mind, I was at first reluctant to relinquish the plan I had for the sixth book, but then gradually what my friends were saying seemed to make more and more sense. Once my decision was made, I suddenly felt very much lighter. With my broad-based book on Adoption, Fostering and Step Families still to complete, I realised that I had quite enough big projects on my plate and that here I had something I could dispatch much more easily and quickly!

But before I dispatch it, I feel that a few further words about Helen Weaver (Munro) and her healing (which is also of course my own) are called for. Percy M. Young wrote a book about Alice Elgar, and more recently the playwright Peter Sutton drew attention to "the other Alice in EE's life."[6] I have already mentioned John E. Kelly's interesting book about EE's great friend Alfred Rodewald, upon whom he depended for a short time for advice on some of his composing, and now too even Troyte Griffith, EE's architect friend, who is number seven in the *Enigma Variations*, has been commemorated in a biography ably written by Professor Jeremy Hardie.[7] Also, besides his book about Elgar's *last* love mentioned in my Acknowledgements, Kevin Allen has recently published an enormous book[8] about EE's friends, the Norbury sisters of Sherridge (near Malvern), and I have heard that he has a second volume about them on the way. So is it not Helen's turn at last to be given a voice of her own? Cora Weaver, following the extensive research that she carried out in New Zealand, gave us the bones, for which I have already expressed my gratitude; now I hope to have put flesh onto them. Or should I perhaps rather say that (even if they now need some correction) Cora has given us the externals while I have expressed the internals.

Helen has been such a shadowy figure ever since her departure from Worcester to New Zealand; much uncertainty has been expressed about her reasons for emigrating, and its effect on EE and his music has not been fully recognised either. Although EE says in the letter dated 12 March 1906 that he would never disclose Helen's identity, he did in fact divulge his continued feelings for her to his close friend Ivor Atkins, not more than a year or so before he died. See, for instance, David Owen Norris' notes to the Avie 2 CD set of EE's Songs and Piano Music played on Elgar's 1844 Broadwood Square Piano. Yet only during this month of June 2013, Radio 3 broadcast within ten days of each other both the *Enigma Variations* and EE's violin concerto and in neither case was Helen's name mentioned even as a possible subject in EE's mind when he firstly put the asterisks against Variation number XIII and secondly declared the concerto to enshrine somebody's soul! Incidentally, although neither Michael Kennedy nor Cora Weaver mentions Kenneth and EE having met, David Owen Norris' above-mentioned notes do mention it as more or less certain, and he believes this meeting to have had a significant effect on EE. I read these notes only *after* having seen the correspondence about it between Kenneth and his mother in my regression, which of course makes me even more inclined to believe in their having made each other's acquaintance.

Writing about the *Enigma Variations* Michael Kennedy discusses the identity of Variation number XIII at length, if not totally conclusively, and he quotes Ernest Newman, who seemed *sure* that it was Helen Weaver. While not himself displaying a hundred per cent conviction on the matter, Kennedy says, "The music, at any rate, is full of dream-like regret" – not a thing that EE had any reason to feel over Lady Mary Lygon's temporary absence on a sea voyage! As for the Violin concerto, when EE made the whisper quoted by Kevin Allen he was obviously thinking about Vera but when he was actually writing the Concerto I am quite sure that he was thinking about Helen Weaver. So, whether or not anyone else accepts my personal conviction, I feel happy at having the chance to declare to the world of music that the love between EE and Helen Weaver was both real and enduring, and that it served a purpose in his work as well as in her spiritual development.

We often make rational decisions during our lives and there is nothing wrong with that. When a rational decision is made in accordance with what our heart is saying too, the outcome can normally be expected to be as near perfect as is humanly possible. When, however, the heart is suppressed or ignored in favour of a decision that is primarily rational, the heart will eventually protest – even if it takes a very long time about it. Helen did, I believe, an excellent job in making a new life for herself on the other side of the world and, according to my personal belief system, she did it partly because she knew subconsciously that Alice was the wife best suited to enabling EE to achieve all that he did. I can see clearly now that it was that sub-conscious knowledge that prevented me as a besotted teenager from feeling any jealousy of my 'beloved's' wife. Helen's *heart*, however, never recovered from losing that great love and she had to come into a new body in order to repair that.

I have mentioned the fact that the most important work that we do in DMP is after the death, in the *Bardo*, and here two of the most important questions that the therapist asks are normally, "Which aspects of this character and her experiences are you now ready to let go of?" and "What of her life will it be beneficial for you to retain?" So now I, as Ann, feel Helen's legacy inside me, and her great love of music is the most important part of that. I also delight in having finally found an explanation for the unusual feelings that I have had for EE since adolescence. And, having found that explanation as well as clarifying her feelings to my personal satisfaction, I am ready to let go of her grief, her constant wish for "something better", for something that she could have had "if only…" I think she *did* find some happiness in her life with the good, reliable, John Munro in New Zealand, but that she lacked there the romance and the musical and other fun which she had shared – albeit briefly – with EE. All this helps me now, as Ann, to follow my heart rather than my head whenever possible, to accept and appreciate every detail and aspect of the life that *I* (no longer Helen) have at present and, though ever conscious of the distance there may still be to go, to be grateful for all that I have learnt in this lifetime. Now too I firmly believe that everything is exactly as it is meant to be.

As I sit typing here at my desk in my little study in Ludlow I can, whenever I pause for thought, look up at the photo of the young EE which, thanks to the Birthplace Museum, whose archivist kindly emailed a copy of it to me for my personal use, now hangs framed on my wall. The forget-me-nots that I picked in France just after my regression to the lifetime as Helen, and then pressed, now have a place above the frame, reminding me of the picture I got of EE picking a little bunch of those flowers for her. EE's moustache is dark and large (it must have tickled when we kissed!), his cheek is resting on his lightly clenched left hand, and his dreamy gaze is directed not at me – nor even, I think, at either of the Alices or Vera (who was to come into his life only very much later) – but into eternity. An eternity in which there will always be music that has come from and goes to the heart. An eternity in which he and his music will always have an important part.

Some people might say that, since before long it will be eighty years since he departed this Earth, has EE not yet returned into a new incarnation. Well, it seems that there are no rules about the amount of time that we spend in between each of our many lives; it depends upon many different factors, including the circumstances in which we will do best at what we still need to learn. Not being clairvoyant, I can only say what I *feel* about what has happened with EE's spirit. So what I feel is that his work as EE is not yet quite complete. The cancer killed his body, but not his soul and, since his return to a higher realm he has had much to do: overseeing the completion of his third symphony was one important thing, encouraging other countries that have yet to recognise his greatness to perform his works is another. And now I feel strongly that it is he who has been urging me on while I have been putting this little book together – at much greater speed than any of my previous books. Although he was only two years old when his family moved from Lower Broadheath back into Worcester, he always cared greatly for the place, and as children he and his brothers used to holiday on a nearby farm. I know for sure that he now cares greatly about the Birthplace Museum and its welfare, as well as the people who look after both it and his family's adjacent cottage, which his daughter Carice secured for the nation. I believe too that that is why, on 18 May 2013, he gave me such a big kick to put onto paper what had been brewing in the back of my mind for a full year. I just hope and pray that he will feel satisfied with my efforts!

Notes

1. *OUTLIERS – The Story of Success*, Malcolm Gladwell, Penguin, 2009.

2. *BLINK – The Power of Thinking without Thinking*, Malcolm Gladwell, Penguin, 2006.

3. *THE FABER POCKET GUIDE TO BACH*, Sir Nicholas Kenyon, Faber and Faber, 2011.

4. *BACH: Essays on his Life and Music*, Christoph Wolff, Harvard University Press, 1994

5. *THE POWER OF MODERN SPIRITUALITY*, William Bloom, Piatkus, 2011

6. Peter Sutton's delightful play, *Alice and Elgar*, was written for the 150th centenary of the composer's birth. I am grateful to his work for introducing me to the importance of Alice Stuart Wortley in EE's life.

7. *Troyte Griffith: Malvern Architect and Friend of Elgar*, Jeremy Hardie, Aspect Design, 2012. This beautiful, copiously illustrated book, is on sale at the Elgar Birthplace Museum

8. *GRACIOUS LADIES: The Norbury Family and Edward Elgar*, Kevin Allen, 2013.

Ann and her husband on the J. S. Bach Journey, 2013

The Elgar family graves at St Wulstan's, near Malvern, Worcs.

The grave of the two dogs, Marco and Mina, who survived Elgar. Carice, who took them over after his death, had them buried in the garden of the Birthplace cottage

By the same author

Discovering the Life Plan – Eleven Steps to your Destiny, O-Books, 2012. ISBN 978-84694-821-3
Delayed Departure – A Beginner's Guide to Soul Rescue, O-Books, 2013 ISBN 978-1-78279-011-2

6th Books investigates the paranormal, supernatural, explainable or unexplainable. Titles cover everything included within parapsychology: how to, lifestyles, beliefs, myths, theories and memoir.